Grade 3: Table of

Grade 3: Introduction

Exercise is an important part of a healthy lifestyle. By exposing children to a variety of activities, games, and sports, we are giving them an opportunity to choose the exercise that fits their personal needs. Some students may enjoy being in groups and may be good runners. They might choose to participate in team sports like soccer or lacrosse. Others, who also like to run, may prefer simply to challenge themselves. They may pursue cross-country track. However, before students choose an activity, they need to learn about different events so they can find out what skills they are good at and which ones they enjoy. As educators, we can provide students with the opportunity to practice those skills in a fun and stress-free environment.

High Interest Sports introduces a variety of games and sports to students. It is designed so that both boys and girls can benefit from the lessons. Moreover, students learn about famous people, past and present, who have enhanced some of the sports. The activity sheets will provide students with a working knowledge of different sports with the expectation that they can try some of the skills. However, *High Interest Sports* is not intended as a rules book. By exploring different sports, students might be encouraged to begin a life program of exercise in a fun, fulfilling venue.

Organization

High Interest Sports is divided into three units.

- **Games with Class:** This unit reviews nine games popular on school playgrounds. The games include such favorites as kickball, jump rope, and tetherball.

- **On Your Own:** The second unit examines sports individuals compete in, such as swimming, downhill skiing, and skateboarding. Some of the people students read about are Mark Spitz and Jesse Owens.

- **Teaming Up:** The last unit explores both the popular team sports as well as the lesser-known ones. Students learn about football, volleyball, and luge racing. They meet such superstars as John Elway and Wayne Gretzky.

Each sport topic is designed as a two-page lesson. The first page explains the basic rules, equipment, and play of the game in a fun and interesting format. The details may be written in a letter, an Internet site, or a "you are there" scenario. Readability of these stories ranges from 2.2 to 3.1. The second page of each lesson serves as an assessment to review important details covered in the story. The assessment formats include multiple choice, analogy, fill in the blank, definition, comparison, and crossword puzzles.

Grade 3: Introduction

Use

Students do not need additional instruction to complete any of the pages in this book. Copies of the activity sheets can be given to individuals, pairs of students, or small groups for completion. They can also be used as a center activity.

To begin, determine the implementation that best fits your students' needs and your classroom structure. The following plan suggests a format for this implementation:

1. Explain the purpose of the activity sheets to your class. Let them know that the activities will be fun as well as helpful.

2. Review the mechanics of how you want the students to work with the activity sheets. Do you want them to work in groups? Are the activities for homework?

3. Introduce students to the process and to the purpose of the activity. Go over the directions. Work with children when they have difficulty. Give only a few lessons at a time.

4. Follow each lesson with a class discussion. Encourage students to share what they have learned from each lesson. If possible, have students try some of the skills associated with the sport. Perhaps students would like to role-play some of the skills.

5. Most importantly, encourage the children to have fun. They should enjoy this time of discovery and exploration.

Additional Notes

Parent Letter: Send the Letter to Parents home with students.

Sports Survey: On page 5, there is a survey students can take to examine how they view sports. You may want to have students fill out the survey prior to beginning the lessons. Then have them put the page in their portfolio. At another point in the year, have students take the survey again. They can compare it to their first survey to see if their views and attitudes have changed with exposure to a wide variety of sports.

Good Sportsmanship: Students hear many times the importance of being a good sport. Page 6 briefly reviews the concepts associated with sportsman-like behavior.

The President's Challenge: The President's Challenge is a fitness program started in 1965 as a way to encourage students to practice a healthy lifestyle. It is a program that only certified PE teachers may test. However, pages 7-8 explain the basic concepts of the program to students. For more information, contact The President's Challenge at 1-800-258-8146 to order the necessary information.

Gold Medal Award: Page 95 has four awards that recognize students' behavior in team situations. These awards include Good Sport, Team Helper, Team Cheerleader, and Team Player of the Day. Copy the page on yellow paper, cut out the "medals," and staple each to a ribbon. Give the awards to your students to let them know that they are gold-medal players—on and off the playground.

Dear Parent,

Exercise is an important part of a healthy lifestyle. By exposing children to a variety of exercises, activities, and games, we are giving them the opportunity to choose the exercise that fits their individual needs, talents, and skills. Some children may choose team sports, while others may choose individual running events. However, children need to be exposed to a variety of sports to learn the kinds of skills necessary to perform the activity before they can choose.

During the year, your child will explore a variety of games and sports through activity sheets. The games include classroom activities such as four square and tetherball, and sports like swimming and soccer. Your child will also read about some of the people who have excelled in these arenas. From time to time, I may send home worksheets, whether completed in class or to be completed at home. To help your child progress at a faster rate, please consider the following suggestions:

- *Together, review the work your child brings home or completes at home.*

- *Encourage your child to try some of the skills associated with the games he or she reads about.*

- *Guide your child to see why it is important to have a healthy lifestyle.*

- *Play with your child and have fun!*

Thank you for your help. Your child and I appreciate your assistance and reinforcement in this learning process.

Cordially,

A Sporting Chance

Answer the questions below.

1. What do you like to do?

_____

_____

_____

2. What are you good at doing?

_____

_____

_____

3. Do you like to play games that you play alone or with people? Why?

_____

_____

_____

4. What games would you like to learn more about?

_____

_____

_____

A Name in Sports

Wayne Gretzky is an ice hockey player. He has helped his team win many games. People call him "The Great One." Wayne got this name for being a good player—both on the ice and off the ice. He is kind to the people on his team. He talks nicely about the people on the other team. He also likes to talk with the people who come to watch the games. Wayne is a good sport!

There are many kinds of teams. There are teams in sports. There are teams to work on class work. There are even teams to practice spelling words. A team can have two or more people. Playing on a team can be hard. Everybody gets a turn. Sometimes, one person can do a better job than his or her teammates. Being a good sport means that you have to think about how other people feel. A good sport makes all the players feel good about the job they do.

Being a good sport is not easy. It takes practice. Here are some ways that you can be a good sport:

★ Talk nicely to everyone at the game. This means players on both teams and people watching the game.

★ Talk nicely about the people on your team.

★ Talk nicely about the people on the other team.

★ Before players take a turn, talk to them. Tell them they will do a good job.

★ When players are done, talk to them again. If they did not do well, say they will do better next time.

★ Help other players who might like to learn to do a better job.

★ Keep a smile on your face—no matter what happens in the game.

★ If you did something really well, everyone already knows. Talking about it a lot might make other people feel bad.

There are many other ways to be a good sport. Keep your eyes and ears open. Then maybe the people on your team will call you "The Great One." You can be like Wayne Gretzky.

Fit for Life

Do you exercise every day? Do you eat foods that are good for you? Getting exercise and eating the right foods are good ways to stay healthy. You will feel better. You will also have less chance to get sick.

Your school can help you exercise and eat good foods. At lunch, the cafeteria serves the food you need. Some schools even serve breakfast. You need the food. Food is like the gas in a car. Food gives you energy. It helps you to think and move.

The muscles in your body need to exercise once they get food. Muscles are groups of tissues. There are many kinds of muscles. Your arms and legs have muscles to make your body move. Your heart is a muscle, too. By moving your whole body, you exercise many muscles. Your teacher gives you time to exercise all these muscles. Sometimes you may go outside. Just running and jumping is good for you. Your teacher may also show you how to play games. During these games, you will learn how to kick, throw, jump, and run faster.

Some schools have a PE teacher. This teacher may ask you take a fitness test. It is a special test that many students around the United States take. It is called "The President's Challenge." Students between the ages of 6 and 17 can take the test. There are five exercises that you must do. Everybody can do the exercises. If you have special needs, there are exercises you can do. You take the test twice each year—once at the beginning of the school year and again at the end of the year. By doing the test twice, you can practice during the year. You can do a better job. If you do a really good job, you can get an award.

You will have fun doing The President's Challenge. It will help you learn how to be healthy. Just remember to do your best. You will be surprised at how well you do! Then you can be fit for life.

Go on to the next page.

Fit for Life, p. 2

The President's Challenge tests five exercises. The list here will help you practice for the test. However, your PE teacher will show you the best way to do each exercise. Remember to stretch before you begin any exercise.

Curl-Ups

Curl-ups test the muscles in your stomach. You lie on the floor on your back. Then you pull your knees up. Your feet should stay flat on the floor. A friend holds your feet. Now, cross your arms. How many times can you touch your elbows to your knees in one minute?

Shuttle Run

The shuttle run sees how fast you can run. You will need two blocks or erasers. Place the blocks about 30 feet away. Have a friend use a clock to time you. Run to pick up the first block. Bring it back to the start line. Run to get the other block. Have your friend stop the clock when you bring the second eraser to the start line.

One Mile Run/Walk

This exercise is good for your heart and lungs. You run or walk a mile. You want to go as fast as you can because you are racing against the clock. You will need to work on this exercise several times each week. It is hard to go that far unless you are in good shape. Also, be sure to practice in a safe place, away from cars and bikes.

Pull-Ups

Pull-ups test the muscles in your arms. If your playground has bars, you can practice this exercise at school. Hold the bar so that you can see your knuckles. Hang on the bar so your feet do not touch the floor. Now pull your body up. Have your chin go over the bar. Move your body down. How many can you do?

V-Sit Reach

This exercise tests how well you can bend. You sit on the floor. Put your legs out in front of you. Your legs should be about ten inches apart. Hold your thumbs together. Put your arms out in front of you between your legs. Now reach as far as you can. Be sure not to bend your knees.

UNIT 1: Games with Class

Get Your Kicks Here!

The score is tied, with four runs for each team. Your team has two outs. No one is on base. It is your turn to kick the ball. You need a home run so that your team can win the game. The ball rolls to home plate. You kick the ball hard. It flies over the heads of the pitcher and second baseman. You run as fast as you can to all three bases. You are now running to home plate. Hurry, here comes the ball! SAFE!

Kickball is a favorite game for all ages. A kickball field has three bases and a home plate. The field is shaped like a diamond. To play, you only need a rubber ball and base markers. Two teams play the game. Most teams are made up of nine players, but you just need to have the same number of people on each team. One team kicks, and the other team plays in the field. The team in the field tries to catch the ball and get the kicking team out. A team has three outs. The teams trade places after three outs. The team with the most points at the end of the game wins.

Suppose your class is playing another kickball game. Your team is kicking first. The pitcher from the other team rolls the ball to home plate. You get three chances to kick the ball. If you miss the ball or the ball rolls past the foul line, it counts as a chance. When you kick the ball, you must run to first base as fast as you can. Watch the other team! There are three ways they can get you out. One way is that the ball gets to first base before you do. Also, someone on the other team can catch the "fly" ball you kicked high into the air before it hits the ground. Finally, you can get out if someone on the other team tags you with the ball.

There are other rules in kickball. Once on base, you can only run after a teammate kicks the ball and the ball hits the ground. Also, you must run to the next base if a teammate is on the base behind you. However, if there is no one on that base, you don't have to run. When a teammate kicks a fly ball, you must stay on base until the ball hits the ground or the other team catches it. Then you may run to as many bases as you can without being tagged by the ball. As you pass each base, you must touch it with your foot. You score a point, or a run, when you touch home plate.

Now you really know how to put some "kick" into your school day—just run for home!

Go on to the next page.

Get Your Kicks Here!, p. 2

Circle the word or phrase that completes each sentence.

1. A kicker can have _____ chances to kick the ball.
   a. two   **b.** three   **c.** four

2. Each team gets three _____ before the teams change places.
   a. outs   **b.** kicks   **c.**   runs

3. A runner may not go to the next base until _____.
   a. the pitcher rolls the ball
   b. the kicker is out
   c. the ball touches the ground after it is kicked

4. Teams must have _____.
   a. the same number of people
   b. 11 people
   c. the same shirts

5. The team in the field tries to _____.
   a. yell the loudest
   b. run the bases
   c. get the kicking team out

6. A player is out when he or she _____.
   a. is tagged by the ball before reaching base
   b. kicks a ball past the foul line
   c. touches first base

7. A team wins by _____.
   a. having the most players
   b. making the most runs
   c. getting the most outs

Take Your Turn!
Kickball is similar to baseball. Research both
games to find out how they are alike and different.

This Game Is "Four" Squares

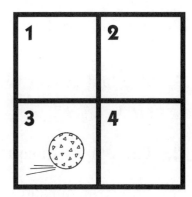

"Keisha, why is the class standing in line on the playground?" Todd asked.

"They are waiting to play foursquare. See the four squares on the ground? Each square has a number in it. A player stands in each square. The players bounce a rubber ball to each other. The goal of the game is to get to square 1. When you are in square 1, you get to start the game each time," said Keisha.

Todd watched the game. Dan stood in square 1. He held the ball. Rachel stood in square 2. Tom was in square 3, and Jan was in square 4.

"Let's play," said Dan. He pushed the ball with his hand. It bounced in square 3 to Tom. Tom sent the ball to Rachel in square 2.

"Line," called Rachel.

Tom smiled and laughed. "I'm out! Jan, you get to move to square 3." Tom walked to the end of the line.

"Keisha, why did Tom go to the end of the line?" asked Todd.

"In foursquare, if the ball hits the line or bounces outside of the square, the last player to touch the ball is out. Players are also out if the ball bounces in their square, and they miss the ball. Players who are out must go to the end of the line to wait for a turn to play again. The players who are in the squares with the higher numbers move to the next square. The first person waiting in line will get to play in square 4," said Keisha.

Sonya walked into square 4. Dan started another game. He bounced the ball to square 2. Rachel sent the ball back to Dan. He bounced it right back to Rachel. Next, Rachel bounced it to Sonya in square 4. She quickly sent it to Dan. It bounced inside the square. Dan could not get the ball. It bounced out.

Rachel raised her arms in glee. "Dan, I am sorry that you are out, but I am also glad! Now I can be in square 1 and start the game," she said.

"Enjoy it while you can, Rachel. I will be back," he laughed.

The players on the court moved. Keisha walked to square 4.

"Good luck," yelled Todd. "Now I want to play. I am all 'four' this game!"

Go on to the next page.

Name _____ Date _____

This Game Is "Four" Squares, p. 2

Use words from the Word List to complete the sentences.

Word List
- walks
- line
- four
- square
- one
- hands
- bounce
- out

1. The last player to touch the ball is out when the ball lands on a _____ .

2. The player in square _____ starts the game.

3. The first person waiting in line moves to square _____ when he or she begins to play.

4. Players _____ the ball to each other.

5. Players want to get the person in square 1 _____ .

6. Players who miss the ball after it bounces in their _____ are out.

7. Players hit the ball with their _____ .

8. When a player gets out, he or she _____ to the end of the line to wait for another turn.

Take Your Turn!

Make a foursquare court and get a rubber ball. Ask your friends to play foursquare with you.

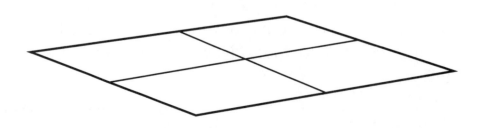

All Wrapped Up!

Dear Soon-Li,

I am visiting my grandmother during spring break. I am having so much fun! She lives near a park. All the children in the neighborhood meet there every day. I have made many new friends. I have also learned to play a new game. It is called tetherball. Let me tell you how to play this game.

The court has a long pole in the center. A rope ties a ball to the pole. Two people play at a time. Other people who want to play must wait in line for their turn. The goal of the game is to hit the ball over the head of the other player so that the rope wraps all the way around the pole. The first player to do this wins. The winner stays on the court and will play the next person in line. The other person must go to the end of the line to wait for his or her turn to play again.

Tetherball sounds easy, but it is harder than you think! You get one half of the court, and you cannot cross sides. You can only hit the ball with one hand. Some players always use their fist. Other players hit the ball with their hand open. You must be careful not to push the ball, though. It is called a "carry" if you do. Also, you can only hit the ball one time when it is on your half of the court. You cannot hit it again until the other player has touched it. Finally, you cannot touch the rope. If you do any of these things, you are out and must go to the end of the line to wait for another turn.

When I first started playing tetherball, I always lost. Now that I play the game every day, I win a lot. I think the whole class will like this game. Maybe we can get our school to make a tetherball court for us!

I will be home next week. Tell everyone I said "hi."

Your friend,
Gina

Go on to the next page.

All Wrapped Up!, p. 2

Circle the word that has the same or similar meaning to the word or words in bold type.

1. A tetherball court is made by tying a ball to a tall **stick**.
   a. tape   **b.** tree   **c.** pole

2. Two **people on the court** can play at a time.
   a. players   **b.** friends   **c.** balls

3. You can hit the ball with your **hand closed** or with your hand open.
   a. fist   **b.** glove   **c.** fingers

4. If you touch the **string**, you are out.
   a. ball   **b.** player   **c.** rope

5. You win if you can **wind** the ball all the way around the pole.
   a. swing   **b.** blow   **c.** wrap

6. The winner **begins** the next game.
   a. ends   **b.** starts   **c.** wins

7. Players get one **time** to hit the ball when it is in their court.
   a. chance   **b.** game   **c.** hand

Take Your Turn!

How much would it cost to make a
tetherball court at your school?
Research to find out this information.

Caution: Obstacles Ahead!

An obstacle is something that is in your way. It blocks the way you want to go. In an obstacle course, you choose a path to follow in which there are things to move around, under, over, in, and through. Most of the time, you must move in different ways, like hopping or skipping backwards, to get to each obstacle. At the same time, you can use balls, hoops, ropes, and playground equipment, like slides. Obstacle courses can be set up inside a classroom or outside on a playground.

To set up an obstacle course, choose a start and finish line. Think about the age of the players and what kinds of moves they can safely do. Then decide what obstacles you will use. How will your friends move from obstacle to obstacle? Will you need balls or ropes? Here are some ideas of things you may want to do when you make an obstacle course.

★ Hop, skip, jump rope, or crab-walk between obstacles.
★ Dribble a ball between obstacles.
★ Crawl under a table.
★ Slide down a slide.
★ Throw a beanbag into a box.
★ Jump through a hula hoop.
★ Roll a ball with a bat.
★ Walk with a book on your head.

Safety is very important in an obstacle course. Here are some things to keep in mind when you set up. Look for a dry, clean place. It is easy to fall on wet surfaces. Think about the people who run your course. Choose obstacles and ways to move that all the players can do. Do not use obstacles in which players jump from high places.

Once your course is set up, show the players how to do it. Then let them try it once. It will help them remember what to do. When the game begins, have players start when the person before them has started the third obstacle. When they cross the finish line, players should move away from the line.

Go on to the next page.

Caution: Obstacles Ahead!, p. 2

Circle the word that completes the analogy.

1. blocks : path   obstacle : _____
   a. build   **b.** course   **c.** walk

2. inside : classroom   outside : _____
   a. playground **b.** slide   **c.** library

3. _____ : ball   jump : rope
   a. swing   **b.** round   **c.** dribble

4. dirty : _____   wet : dry
   a. brown   **b.** water   **c.** clean

5. crawl : under   jump : _____
   a. over   **b.** hop   **c.** rope

6. start line: begin   finish line: _____
   a. done   **b.** end   **c.** draw

Take Your Turn!

Look at your playground. Make an obstacle course for your classmates to try. Will you need balls or ropes? How will the players move between the obstacles? Remember, make an obstacle course that everyone can do!

Hop and Jump

Hopscotch is a funny name
For a hopping, jumping game.
Draw nine squares as shown below.
Get a rock so you can go.
Wait in line to take a turn.
See what you can watch and learn.
You have to jump to number 9
Without stepping on a line.

Toss your rock in the first square.
Hop with one foot in the air.
Hop in 2 and then in 3,
Then look at 4 and 5 to see—
These two squares are double wide.
Jump with your feet side by side.
Hop in 6, jump in 7 and 8
Don't stop now; You are doing great!
Hop once more to number 9
I see you didn't touch a line.
Keep your foot up in the air.
And turn around in this square.

Don't you like to play this game?
Go back again, just like you came,
But stop in 2 and bend right down—
Keep hands and one foot off the ground.
Get your rock and you are done,
After hopping in square 1.
Wait in line to go once more.
Then toss your rock just like before.
Have it land in the next square.
Outside the box is just not fair.
When your rock lands in square 9,
And you make it back just fine,
You do not have to go again,
Because you played nine rounds to win!

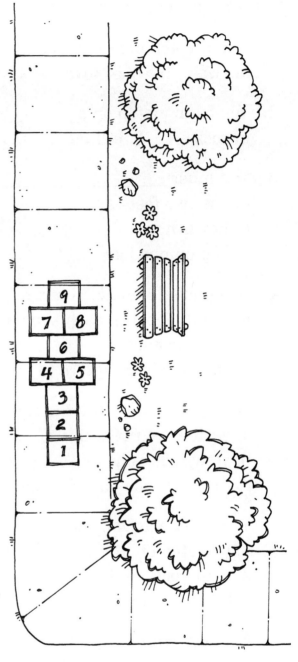

Go on to the next page.

Hop and Jump, p. 2

Circle the word or phrase that completes each sentence.

1. A hopscotch board is made with _____ squares.
   a. two   **b.** seven   **c.** nine

2. You cannot step on a _____.
   a. rock   **b.** line   **c.** number

3. You must _____ in square 3.
   a. use two feet
   b. never hop
   c. hop on one foot

4. In squares 7 and 8, you can _____.
   a. put one foot in each square
   b. turn around
   c. choose which square to jump into

5. You do not jump into the square _____.
   a. with a 1 written in it
   b. your rock is in
   c. that is beside another square

6. You must wait for another turn if _____.
   a. you step on a line
   b. your rock lands outside the square you are playing for
   c. both **a** and **b**

7. A player wins by _____.
   a. jumping up and back nine times
   b. finishing nine rounds
   c. tossing a rock into square 9

Take Your Turn!

Find some chalk. Draw a hopscotch board in a safe place outside. Find a rock or another marker, like a penny. Can you keep your balance when you hop?

Jump for Joy!

Jumping rope is a favorite game. It is also a great way to get exercise. It makes you move many different parts of your body at the same time. You can play alone or with a group. All you need is a rope and a safe space to swing it.

At first, it may be hard to swing your arms and jump with both feet at the same time. The rope may get caught on your feet. Sometimes the rope can get caught on your shoulders. Don't give up! It takes a lot of practice.

Here is a checklist of different jump-rope tricks you can do. Try each one several times. See how many you can do. Record your best try.

1. Jump with two feet Best try: _____	**2.** Hop on one foot Best try: _____
3. Jump very fast Best try: _____	**4.** Jump while running Best try: _____
5. Bounce two times Best try: _____	**6.** Switch feet while hopping Best try: _____

Now that you know some jumping tricks, use them in new ways. You can turn on some music. Is the music fast or slow? Jump to the beat of the music. You might even want to make up a jump-rope dance to the music. You can teach it to your friends.

Next, get a longer rope. Ask two friends to turn it for you. Practice the same tricks that you have already learned. Tell your friends if they need to turn the rope faster or slower for you. Make sure that you give your friends a turn to jump!

There are many other ways to jump! Some people like to chant. Some people use two long ropes at the same time when they jump. Try to find some new ways to jump.

Go on to the next page.

Unit 1: Games with Class
 High Interest Sports 3, SV 3822-0

Jump for Joy, p. 2

Complete the puzzle.

Across

2. You jump with your _____.
4. You turn the rope with your _____.
5. You must _____ to become a good rope jumper.
6. Different ways to jump rope are called _____.

Down

1. You need _____ to swing the rope safely.
3. Jumping rope is good _____.
7. To play this game, all you need is a _____.

Take Your Turn!

Double Dutch is a way to jump rope. People work in teams to play. The teams can go to play with other teams. Judges choose which is the best team. Research to find out what Double Dutch jumping is and how to do it.

Float to Fun

What is a parachute?

A parachute is a fun piece of equipment for you and your friends to play with. It is a circle made of many colors. It looks like a colorful pie. There is a hole in the middle. You will need many friends to play games with it.

How does a parachute work?

The parachute is made of a very thin cloth. When you lift the parachute and pull it down, the cloth fills with air. It looks like a big mushroom. It takes a while for the air to go out of the parachute.

What games can you play with a parachute?

Popcorn	*Mushroom*	*Inside a Mushroom*
Hold the parachute around the edges while standing. Lift the parachute so it is waist-high. Throw several small balls, like tennis balls, onto the parachute. Work together to shake the balls out.	Lay the parachute on the ground. Stand around the outside. Bend over and hold onto the parachute. Count to 3. When everyone says 3, lift the parachute high into the air. Pull it down to the ground quickly. Place your hands and knees on the edges to keep the air inside. Count out loud together to find how long the parachute stays up.	Lay the parachute on the ground. Stand around the outside. Bend over and hold onto the parachute. Count to 3. When everyone says 3, lift the parachute high into the air. As the parachute is pulled down, take a step forward. Pull the edges down behind your back. Sit down on the edge of the parachute.

Go on to the next page.

Unit 1: Games with Class
High Interest Sports 3, SV 3822-0

Float to Fun, p. 2

✎ **Write** the word that completes each sentence.

1. A _____ is shaped like a circle.

2. A parachute has many colors that make it look like a colorful
_____.

3. When a parachute is filled with air, it looks like a big
_____ .

4. Balls bouncing in the parachute look like _____ .

Answer the question.

5. What do you think it looks like when you sit inside a parachute?

_____

_____

_____

Take Your Turn!
Research to find how parachutes
were first used.

This Race Is a Tie

Mr. Nixon looked around the classroom as he talked. Some of the students were looking out the window. Others had their heads on their desks. Raul, who was always a good listener, was reading a book. Even Mr. Nixon felt bored. Yes, it was time for a class break! Mr. Nixon closed his book with a snap.

"Line up!" he said. Surprised, the class walked to the door. Mr. Nixon pulled a bag out of his desk. The class walked quickly outside.

"Find a partner. We are going to try running a three-legged race," said Mr. Nixon. He pulled long pieces of cloth from the bag. He gave each pair of students a piece of cloth.

"Stand beside your partner. Then tie the cloth around two legs—one leg from each person," Mr. Nixon said. "Don't tie it so hard that the cloth will hurt. Now, work with your partner to walk."

Mr. Nixon laughed out loud as he watched the class. Rosa and Joan kept hitting each other with their arms. They laughed loudly as they tried to walk. John and Eric kept falling down. John was very tall. Eric was much shorter. Each time they walked, they fell down. John's steps were much bigger than Eric's steps. The boys talked for a few minutes. For the next try, John took smaller steps. Now they were able to walk without falling.

Raul and Dan were doing the best, though. They had an arm around each other. They were also counting quietly, "1, 2, 1, 2." When they said *1*, the boys would move their outside legs. When they counted *2*, they would move their tied legs. Raul and Dan walked quickly around the group. The other students watched how the boys moved. Soon all the partners moved quickly and easily.

Mr. Nixon smiled. "Now, it is race time. Here is the start line and the finish line. Each team will race to the other side of the field and back. Any team that crosses the line is a winner. If you fall, you may get up and keep racing. Now, let's put what we have learned to work."

"Mr. Nixon, we are playing. We are not learning anything," said Rosa.

"Oh, but you are learning many things by doing a three-legged race," Mr. Nixon answered. "You are learning about how your body moves. You are also learning how to work together!"

Go on to the next page.

This Race Is a Tie, p. 2

Circle the word that has the same or similar meaning to the word or words in bold type.

1. **Two people** make a team in a three-legged race.
   a. Friends   **b.** Partners   **c.** Tall

2. A piece of cloth is needed to **join** the legs.
   a. glue   **b.** sew   **c.** tie

3. Be careful not to **pain** the legs by wrapping the cloth too hard.
   a. hit   **b.** kick   **c.** hurt

4. It is important that the two people move their outside feet **at the same time.**
   a. left   **b.** together   **c.** only

5. The arms should be **in back of** the other person.
   a. beside   **b.** hitting   **c.** behind

6. **Saying numbers** will help keep a walking pattern.
   a. Counting   **b.** Adding   **c.** Spelling

7. If you **land on the ground,** you may get up and keep racing.
   a. fly   **b.** walk   **c.** fall

Take Your Turn!

Work with a partner. Try to walk on "three" legs.

UNIT 2: On Your Own

A Zigzag Trail

Just imagine you are on a tall mountain. It is very steep. It looks as if you will fall off the side. All you have to help you get down the mountain are two skis and two poles. The skis are thin strips of metal or wood. The skis help you glide over the ice and snow. The poles are like thin sticks. They help to keep you from falling over.

You see small spots that show a path down the hill. The spots are really flags. These flags show you the course that you must follow to get down the hill. The course is about 1/4 mile long. You see, you are a downhill skier. Just like a runner in a hurdle race, you must get past things that are in your way. You will ski in and out of the flags, called gates. The gates are placed 10 to 15 feet apart. They mark a path that will take you from one side of the mountain to the other. Men have 55 gates and women have 45 gates. While skiing, you may not knock a gate down. You may not miss skiing around any gates. You will be out of the race if you do.

You place the ski goggles, or plastic glasses, over your eyes. You dig your poles into the snow. All at once, you push your body forward. You dig the poles once more into the snow. You keep your body low. Your back is bent over. This position makes you smaller. The wind will slow you down less. You are racing down the hill. The wind blows in your face. You pick up speed as you go. You must keep your knees together and the top part of your body still. You turn quickly as you come to each gate. As you lean from side to side, the poles help you to keep your balance.

The last few gates are in view. The course is not as steep. You need to hurry. There is not much time left if you want to win. The winner has the fastest time. As you ski past the last gate, you dig the poles into the ground. You push your body forward one last time. You made it. Your time was under two minutes. No one can beat that time!

Go on to the next page.

A Zigzag Trail, p. 2

Circle the word that completes the analogy.

1. bat : ball   ski : _____
   a. pole   **b.** boots   **c.** flags

2. rubber : ball   _____ : skis
   a. thin   **b.** glide   **c.** metal

3. runner: hurdle race   skier: _____
   a. poles   **b.** downhill   **c.** mountain

4. bases : plates   gates : _____
   a. flags   **b.** doors   **c.** dishes

5. most : points   _____ : time
   a. fastest   **b.** slowest   **c.** speed

6. tagged with ball: baseball   _____ : downhill skiing
   a. lose a pole   **b.** miss a gate   **c.** low position

Take Your Turn!

The slalom is one kind of Alpine event.
What are the other two? Use the Internet
or other sources to find out.

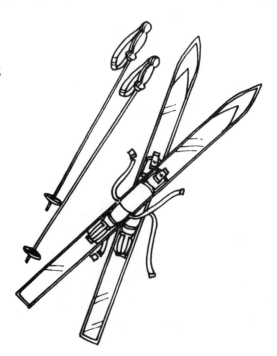

Records in the News

February, 1968
Grenoble, France
◆◆◆◆◆◆◆◆◆◆

SPORTS

Three Wins for France!

Jean-Claude Killy has made Olympic history. He tied a ski record. Jean-Claude won the gold medals in all three snow-skiing events. All the races were close.

In the downhill event, Jean-Claude raced down the hill. The course was a straight path. Some skiers went about 70 miles per hour. Jean-Claude won by .08 seconds. The next race was the giant slalom. The course was longer than the slalom. There were not as many gates. Jean-Claude won the gold medal in this event, too. The final event was the slalom course. Jean-Claude did not have the fastest time. He thought he lost. However, the other two skiers had missed some gates. They could not win. Jean-Claude won after all!

After the races Jean-Claude spoke about his years of training. He

grew up in the French Alps. Jean-Claude was skiing at three years old. He loved to go fast. He loved to speed down the mountains on his skis. He watched many good skiers come train in the mountains near his home. Jean-Claude said, "The best and the fastest way to learn a sport is to watch and imitate a champion." He won his first medal at the age of nine.

Some years have been hard for Jean-Claude to ski. He broke his leg and ankle bones several times. He became sick, too. At one time, Jean-Claude had to stop skiing for two years. He never gave up, though. He worked hard. He pushed himself to do better.

His hard work has helped him to win. France is very proud of their hero! •

Go on to the next page.

Records in the News, p. 2

Circle the word or phrase that completes each sentence.

1. Jean-Claude Killy was a _____.
   a. coach   **b.** ice-skater   **c.** snow-skier

2. He won _____ gold medals in the Olympics.
   a. two   **b.** three   **c.** four

3. His wins were important because _____.
   a. he won all the ski events
   b. he had the fastest times in all events
   c. he was born in France

4. Jean-Claude said that the fastest way to learn a sport was by
   _____.
   a. watching a champion
   b. working hard
   c. reading a book

5. He could not train for two years because _____.
   a. he broke his back
   b. he broke his foot
   c. he was sick

6. While growing up, Jean-Claude loved to
   _____.
   a. race down the mountains on skis
   b. climb the mountains
   c. watch the snow fall on the mountains

Take Your Turn!
Who has the fastest downhill time? Use the
Internet or other sources to find out.

Swimming Is a Cool Sport

Swimming is a great way to cool down on a hot, sunny day. Young children and older adults both enjoy this sport. Many people wear a swimsuit, but others just dive into the water wearing their shorts and shirts.

There are many different places to swim. The ocean is a favorite place to swim. It is fun to jump in and out of the waves. However, swimmers at the ocean must be careful. As the waves leave the beach, they are strong. They may pull swimmers with them. Lakes and rivers are other places to swim. For people who cannot get out to these places, many city parks have pools. The water is clear. A pool is like a big bathtub. Some pools are even built inside buildings.

For most people, swimming is a way to have fun. It means getting into the water and splashing around. The swimmers play games, like tag or Marco Polo. They act like fish and hold their breath under the water as long as they can. Other people just like to stand in the water to stay cool.

Other swimmers like to swim because it is a good way to get exercise. They use many body parts to move through the water. These swimmers swim laps. Laps are done when people swim from one end of the pool to the other many times. They swim using different strokes. One stroke is the freestyle. When doing this stroke, swimmers face down in the water. They kick their feet. Their arms move in circles like pedals on a bike. The backstroke is another way to swim. It is just like the freestyle stroke, except swimmers face up.

Sometimes, people like swimming so much, they want to race other people. They practice swimming laps for several hours each day. They practice all year long. They race other teams. Some teams are from other countries. Swimmers get medals if they win.

Staying safe is important when people swim. People who cannot swim strokes should stay in water they can stand in. Also, people should always swim with a partner. Finally, the sun is very hot. The rays can cause a sunburn. A person's skin can turn bright red like a tomato. All swimmers in and out of the water should wear sunscreen lotion.

Go on to the next page.

Swimming Is a Cool Sport, p. 2

✎ **Write** the word that completes each sentence.

1. A _____ is like a big bathtub.

2. Some swimmers act like _____ and hold their breath under the water.

3. The arms in a freestyle stroke move like _____ on a bike.

4. A sunburn can cause someone's skin to turn red like a _____.

Answer the question.

5. What do you like to do when you swim?

_____

_____

_____

Take Your Turn!

Diving is another way people enjoy the water. Some people practice how to dive every day. They get together at pools and dive against each other. The best diver gets a medal. Research to find the names of three famous divers.

A Splash from the Past

Hello from Munich, Germany. I am Fran Fisher, a news reporter. I am giving you the exciting news of the 1972 Olympic games. People from all over the world have come to be in the Olympic games. They have chosen a sport. Each person has worked hard every day for many years to be the best in this sport. They have high hopes of taking home a gold medal.

Mark Spitz is no different! He is a swimmer from California. He has already won six gold medals in these Olympic games. In each race, Mark has swum faster than anyone else in history for these races. He has beaten each time record. Mark is about to start his last race. If he wins this race, he will have seven gold medals. It will be a world record. No other Olympian has won this many gold medals.

While we are waiting for the race to begin, let me give you some facts about Mark Spitz. He started swimming at the age of 2. Mark's dad was his first coach. Soon Mark needed a new coach. The family lived far away from the coach. Mark's mother would drive him early in the morning every day to swim. The family moved so that Mark could be near his coach. Mark would then have more time to practice.

Mark swam all through his years at school. He won many races. He also raced four years ago at the Mexico City Olympics. Mark won four medals there. Now, at the age of 22, he is better than ever. Mark's best strokes are the freestyle and butterfly.

The swimmers are now set to race. The buzzer sounds. The racers dive into the water. The race has started! Can Mark Spitz be the first person in Olympic history to win seven gold medals? He is ahead of the other swimmers. Can he hold on? Mark touches the wall. Yes! Mark Spitz has done it. He beat the time record for this race, too. He has also won another gold medal!

Go on to the next page.

A Splash from the Past, p. 2

Circle the word or phrase that completes each sentence.

1. Mark Spitz was a famous _____.
   a. diver
   b. swimmer
   c. news reporter

2. The Olympics are games for _____.
   a. swimmers
   b. people who live in the United States
   c. people who live all over the world

3. People who want to go to the Olympics practice _____.
   a. every day
   b. once each week
   c. when they feel like it

4. Mark Spitz's best strokes were the _____ and butterfly.
   a. backstroke
   b. freestyle
   c. float

5. Mark Spitz was the first person in Olympic history to win _____ gold medals.
   a. four   **b.** six   **c.** seven

6. In the 1972 Olympics, Mark made Olympic history by _____.
   a. swimming the fastest times for each race
   b. winning the most gold medals
   c. both **a** and **b**

Take Your Turn!
How many medals has Mark Spitz won in all?
Research on the Internet to find out.

On the Right Track

Dear Aunt Maria,

    Camp Fast Track is fun! I am learning so much about the sport of track and field. It is one of the oldest sports in history. It also has about sixty different events. In events, people run, jump, or throw. Men and women do not compete in the same event.

    In the running events, people run on a track. A track is shaped like an oval. It looks like a road. Tracks are usually about 400 meters long. They are divided into lanes, or paths. Most tracks have six or eight lanes. The running events have different distances. The shortest distance is 100 meters. You have to be very fast. The longest distance is the 10,000 meter run. A runner goes 25 times around a track. In running events, the person who has the fastest time is the winner.

    Some of the jumping events are the long jump, high jump, and pole vault. I like the long jump the best. In these field events, people run and then jump. In the high jump, people jump over a bar. Can you imagine jumping over seven feet into the air? The pole vault has a bar, too. But jumpers use a pole to push their bodies into the air so they go over the bar. In jumping events, the people who jump the highest or farthest win.

    I tried some of the throwing events yesterday. The shot put is a metal ball. There are different size balls for men and women to throw. The shot put for men weighs about seven kilograms and about four kilograms for women. It was too heavy for me to get it very far. I also tried to throw the javelin. A javelin looks like a long stick. I got it much farther than the shot put. The people who throw the farthest are the winners in throwing events.

    This letter is getting long. I will tell you more when I get home!

Sincerely,
Albert

Go on to the next page.

On the Right Track, p. 2

Use words from the Word List to complete the sentences.

	Word List
	longest
	kilograms
	pole
	track
	meters
	fastest
	javelin
	jump

1. In track and field events, people run, throw, or

   _____.

2. A _____ is like an oval road.

3. Running events are measured in

   _____.

4. In the long jump, the person with the

   _____ jump is the winner.

5. People throw a _____ in some events.

6. In running events, the person with the _____ time

   wins.

7. A shot put weighs between four and seven _____.

8. One jumping event has people using a _____ to get

   over a bar.

Take Your Turn!

A decathlon is a special kind of
track and field event. Research to
find out what it is. Also, find the
names of three people who have
done this event.

Role Models on the Run

Jesse Owens and Florence Griffith-Joyner are well-known runners. They are the same in many ways. Both were African Americans. Both were Olympic winners. They even won gold medals in the same events. The events were the 100 meters, 200 meters, and relay races. They set records for the best times in each event. They were winners for running. But they were also winners in other ways.

Jesse Owens was born in 1914. He loved to run and jump. He started track in the fifth grade. He trained hard so that he could run faster and jump farther than many people. In college, he had the fastest time in the world in three events. A year later in 1936, he was ready for the Olympics. The Olympics were in Germany. The people in that country did not make African Americans feel welcome. It did not bother Jesse. He ran the fastest he had ever run. He also jumped the farthest. He won four gold medals. The leader of Germany did not talk to Jesse after his wins. Jesse talked and acted kindly to everyone, though. People in the United States thought Jesse was wonderful to act so nicely when he was treated so badly. He became a hero. When Jesse got back home, he started several running clubs. He taught other children how to work hard to reach their goals. He became as successful in work as he was on the track.

Florence Griffith-Joyner was born in 1959. She began running at the age of 7. She ran in some games Jesse Owens started. Florence worked hard and went to the 1984 Olympics. Everyone noticed Florence. She had style. Florence wore long nails and painted them the colors of the United States flag. She wore running clothes that were bright colors. She won a silver medal that year. Florence kept practicing. She worked harder. In 1988, she won three gold medals. In two of the events, the 100 and 200 meters, she broke world and Olympic records. She became known as Flo-Jo. Flo-Jo was the world's fastest woman. She took some time off from running to start a business making bright running clothes. Like Jesse Owens, she was very successful. However, she loved to run. Flo-Jo started to train again. She wanted to run in the 1996 Olympics, but she got hurt. Flo-Jo could not run. Even after ten years, no other woman has run as fast as her 10.49 seconds in the 100 meters.

Go on to the next page.

Name _____ Date _____

Role Models on the Run, p. 2

Circle the word or phrase that completes each sentence.

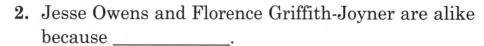

1. _____ holds the world record in the 100 meters.
   a. Jesse Owens
   b. Nellie Bly
   c. Florence Griffith-Joyner

2. Jesse Owens and Florence Griffith-Joyner are alike because _____.
   a. they were runners
   b. they won gold medals in the 100 meters race
   c. both **a** and **b**

3. The people in _____ were not nice to Jesse Owens.
   a. United States
   b. Germany
   c. Canada

4. Jesse won _____ gold medals in the Olympics.
   a. three   **b.** four   **c.** five

5. Flo-Jo liked to wear bright colors of _____.
   a. shoes   **b.** running clothes   **c.** hair

6. After winning Olympic medals, both Jesse and Flo-Jo started _____.
   a. to train for the next Olympics
   b. to learn about other sports
   c. new businesses

Take Your Turn!
If Florence Griffith-Joyner is still considered the world's fastest woman, who is the world's fastest man? Research to find out the name of this person.

Unit 2: On Your Own
High Interest Sports 3, SV 3822-0

Whose Fault Is It?

"That was a fault," said Jana.

"No, it was not a fault," answered Gail.

"The ball hit the line when you served. That makes it a fault. I watch tennis on television. The judges call a fault when the ball hits the line on a serve," said Jana. "Here comes Geraldo. He plays tennis all the time. Geraldo, can you tell us what the rules are in tennis?" Jana asked.

"I see you have the right equipment. You have a racket and tennis balls. You are also wearing clothes that are white or light colors. Your shoes are tennis shoes, too. You now need to know how to play the game," said Geraldo.

"To begin, let's talk about serving the ball. The player who serves the ball gets two tries. The server must stand behind the back line on his or her side of the court. The back line is the baseline. The ball must go over the three-foot net. It must land in the box on the other side of the court. The ball cannot touch any line. The judge calls a fault when these things happen," said Geraldo.

"You were right, Jana," said Gail. "I have much to learn about tennis. What else do I need to know?"

"Players hit the ball back and forth over the net. You want the other player to make a mistake. Then you will score a point. The other player can miss the ball. The ball can bounce two times in the other player's court. Another way to score is if the other player hits the ball outside the court lines or into the net."

"What score do you play to?" asked Gail.

"You have a chance to score four points in each game. Scorekeepers count 15, 30, 40, and then game. In tennis, you must play six games to make a set. Even then, players keep playing. They play matches. In some matches you must win three sets out of five.

"Wow! Tennis is harder than I thought," said Jana. "You can't learn all the rules from watching television."

"Watching tennis on television can be good. You can see how the professional tennis players play. However, you can learn more by playing the game. Why don't we play several games? Then I can help you!" said Geraldo.

Go on to the next page.

Whose Fault Is It?, p. 2

Circle the word or phrase that completes each sentence.

1. The net is _____ high.
   a. 3 feet   **b.** 3 meters   **c.** 3 yards

2. To play tennis, the players hit the ball _____.
   a. into the net
   b. behind the baseline
   c. back and forth over the net

3. A server gets two chances to _____.
   a. bounce the ball
   b. serve the ball
   c. hit the baseline

4. A fault is when _____.
   a. the server misses the ball
   b. a player hits the ball back to the server
   c. the ball lands outside the box on a serve

5. A player scores when _____.
   a. the other player hits the ball out
   b. the other player hits the ball into the net
   c. both **a** and **b**

6. You have to win six games to win a _____.
   a. match   **b.** set   **c.** serve

Take Your Turn!

What is Wimbledon? Research to find out what it is and the names of the players who won last year.

Net Appeal

● Click Here for pictures!

Welcome to the Gabriela Sabatini Internet site.
You will learn about Argentina's favorite tennis star.

Gabriela was six years old. She lived in Buenos Aires, Argentina. She watched her brother play tennis. She wanted to play, too. He gave her an old racket and a tennis ball. Gabriela hit the ball against a wall all day. She was good. She began to take lessons. At the age of ten, she would play games with other people. Some of the other players were much older. Gabriela beat them.

Coach Patricio Apey saw Gabriela play. Gabriela was twelve years old. Coach Apey thought she would be a big tennis star someday. He began to give her lessons. Gabriela left Argentina when she was fourteen. She moved to Florida to train with Coach Apey. She worked hard every day.

At the age of fifteen, Gabriela became a professional tennis player. She went to play at Wimbledon. Wimbledon is an important game for tennis players. People who win at Wimbleton are the best players. Gabriela did not win that year, but she did very well. She was the youngest player to get to the semifinals.

Gabriela kept working hard. She played many tennis games for the next five years. During that time, Gabriela was ranked as one of the top ten women tennis players. Everyone liked Gabriela. She got jobs modeling. She made her own kind of perfume to sell. Gabriela was not totally happy, though. She wanted to win one big tennis game.

In 1990, Gabriela played in the U. S. Open. She had a new coach. She decided to play tennis for fun. Gabriela made it to the final game. She had to play Steffi Graf, another good tennis player. Because she wanted to win, Gabriela told herself that she had to do the best that she could. It was a hard game. Gabriela won!

Gabriela played games for six more years. She had been hurt. She was also not playing her best. In 1996, Gabriela decided to stop playing tennis. She was only twenty-six.

● Home

Go on to the next page.

Net Appeal, p. 2

Complete the puzzle.

Across

3. At Wimbledon, Gabriela was the _____ player to get to the semifinals.

5. Gabriela was born in _____.

6. Gabriela plays _____.

7. She became a _____ tennis player at the age of fifteen.

Down

1. Gabriela _____ the U. S. Open.

2. She moved to Florida when she was _____ years old.

4. Gabriela's _____ gave her a racket and ball to play with.

Take Your Turn!

Who are the top ten men and women tennis players? Research to find out this information.

Taking a Turn

Gymnastics is a sport that requires both power and beauty. Women who do this sport flip forward and backward. They jump in different ways. They add these moves to dances they do. Gymnasts make their moves look easy. But it is really hard to smile and move the body in so many ways.

Women gymnasts have four events. They must do all of them when they compete. One event is the balance beam. The balance beam is a thick piece of wood. It is 10 centimeters wide and 500 centimeters long. It is 120 centimeters high. Gymnasts flip and dance on it. They must have balance. This means gymnasts keep their bodies straight. They do not lean to the left or right as they move. They may lose their balance. They may fall off the balance beam.

The vault is another piece of equipment. It is also called the horse. It looks like a thin table on two legs. It is as tall as the balance beam, but not as long. It is 35 centimeters wide. Gymnasts run to it. They want to have a lot of speed. It gives them a strong jump. A springboard is in front of the vault. When they jump on the board, it helps push their feet high into the air. Their hands push off the vault at the same time. They spin their bodies. They can do many different turns and flips. They land on both feet on the other side of the vault.

Gymnasts also compete on the uneven bars. There are two bars. One bar is low. It is about 148 centimeters high. The high bar is about 228 centimeters high. The gymnasts swing, turn, and flip from bar to bar. They cannot stop as they move.

The last event is the floor exercise. Gymnasts move to music. They jump, dance, leap, and flip. They must use the whole floor during the music.

Judges are people who watch the events. They tell each gymnast how well she did. The judges give a number grade to each gymnast in each event. These grades are scores. They tell the gymnast if she did a good job. The highest score a gymnast can get is 10.0. A gymnast can win two ways. She can win in each event. Also, the scores from all four events are added together. A gymnast can win the competition if she has the highest sum.

Go on to the next page.

Taking a Turn, p. 2

Circle the word that has the same or similar meaning to the word or words in bold type.

1. A **person who does gymnastics** needs power and beauty.
   a. gymnast   **b.** dancer   **c.** girl

2. Gymnasts flip and dance on **thick pieces of wood.**
   a. uneven bars   **b.** vaults   **c.** balance beams

3. They must **not lean left or right** or they can fall off the equipment.
   a. balance   **b.** lie down   **c.** hold still

4. They swing on **high and low bars**.
   a. uneven bars   **b.** vaults   **c.** balance beams

5. Girls turn flips on the **horse**.
   a. uneven bars   **b.** vault   **c.** balance beam

6. Gymnasts **move their bodies to music** in the floor exercises.
   a. leap   **b.** jump   **c.** dance

7. A judge gives each gymnast a **number grade** in each event.
   a. score   **b.** medal   **c.** letter

Take Your Turn!

Men do gymnastics, too. What kind of gymnastics do they do? How are their events different from the women's events? Research to find out.

A Miller Thriller

Who is Shannon Miller?

Shannon Miller is a
gymnast. She jumps,
dances, and flips in her
sport. She must be good in
four different events. She
does the vault and the floor
exercises. Her best events
are the uneven bars and the
balance beam.

When did Shannon start gymnastics?

Shannon started gymnastics when she was five years old. Shannon's
mother took her to Russia when she was eight. Shannon worked with
some of the best coaches in Russia. The coaches said that Shannon would
be a good gymnast. They told her to work hard. When she came back,
Shannon trained six days every week. She also worked hard on her school
work. She made A's.

What did Shannon win?

Shannon did well at every gymnastics meet. A meet is where gymnasts
from many places come together. They compete with each other to see
who can get a high score. Shannon's first big win was in 1991 at the
World Gymnastics Championships. She won two silver medals. The next
year, Shannon went to her first Olympics. Her elbow was hurt. She still
did all of the events. She won two silver and three bronze medals. She
won the most medals of any United States person. Even after the
Olympics, Shannon kept working hard. She won many championships.
She went back to the Olympics in 1996. Shannon won two gold medals.

Shannon still trains and goes to meets. To this day, Shannon has won
more medals than any other woman gymnast in the United States.

Go on to the next page.

A Miller Thriller, p. 2

Use words from the Word List to complete the sentences.

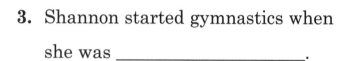

1. Shannon must compete in

   _____ events.

2. Her best events are the uneven bars

   and balance _____.

3. Shannon started gymnastics when

   she was _____.

4. Her mother took her to

   _____ when she was eight.

5. She worked hard in gymnastics

   and _____.

Word List
school
meet
five
Russia
beam
four
medals
elbow

6. A _____ is where gymnasts see who can get high

   scores.

7. During one Olympics, Shannon had a hurt _____.

8. Shannon has won the most _____ of any woman

   gymnast in the United States.

Take Your Turn!

Has any gymnast ever received a 10.0 in an Olympics game? Research to find out.

More Than a Kick

New Karate School Opening Soon!

The Open Hand Karate School will begin lessons next week. Karate means "open hand." Many people think people only do kicks in karate. Karate is a form of exercise. It uses many body parts. Students learn how to move their feet and hands. They learn to jump. There is a kind of karate for every age.

Karate also teaches students how to act. It teaches them to be kind to all people. Karate helps students think about what they do before they act.

Dress

Students will wear white pants and tops. The clothes are loose. Then people can move easily. The top wraps around the body. A white tie belt keeps the top in place. As the students learn to move, they will get a new color belt.

The color of belt shows how much karate a person knows. The highest level is a black belt. People with black belts have taken lessons for many years. During competition, though, people will need to wear white belts. People who do karate do not wear shoes.

Competition

Students will work on a large square mat. Games between two people are called matches. Matches for young students and women last two minutes. Matches last three minutes for men who know the sport. Another person, a referee, is on the mat, too. The referee keeps the people safe. Judges watch each karate match. They give points for how the people look and act. The first person to get three points wins.

Go on to the next page.

45

Unit 2: On Your Own
High Interest Sports 3, SV 3822-0

More Than a Kick, p. 2

Use words from the Word List to complete the sentences.

1. Karate means "open _____."

2. Karate is a good form of _____.

3. The color of the _____ shows how much karate people know.

4. Karate teaches people to be _____.

5. A game between two people is a _____.

6. A _____ makes sure the people are safe.

7. The person who gives points is a _____.

8. The person who scores _____ points first is the winner.

Word List
belt
kind
referee
judge
three
hand
exercise
match

Take Your Turn!

How many colors of belts are there in karate?
Research to find out.

46

Jhoon Rhee's Big Break

I am talking with Jhoon Rhee. He is a tae kwon do master. He was one of the first karate teachers in the United States. I am going to interview him. I have lots of questions to ask.

Interviewer: What is tae kwon do?

Rhee: It is a kind of karate. It is the kind of karate the people in Korea learn. It teaches a way to move the body. It also teaches people how to keep their thoughts together.

Interviewer: When did you learn tae kwon do?

Rhee: I was born in Korea. I learned it from teachers there.

Interviewer: When did you come to the United States?

Rhee: I came to the United States to go to college in 1957.

Interviewer: What made you decide to open a tae kwon do school?

Rhee: The college I went to put on a show. Students could sing, dance, or do other things for fun. I signed up to do some tae kwon do. I showed the people how to break a board with my foot. Many students liked it. They wanted to learn how to break boards, too. So, I started a class. More and more people came to the class. Soon I had to open a school.

Interviewer: How safe is tae kwon do?

Rhee: I make sure my students are safe. I make my students wear special pads. I thought of the ideas for these pads. Students wear the pads on their arms, hands, legs, feet, and heads. It keeps them safe when they kick. But I also teach them the safe way to move their whole body.

Interviewer: Thank you for talking with me, Rhee. That is it for now. Come back again, when I will interview another person who does sports.

Go on to the next page.

Jhoon Rhee's Big Break, p. 2

Circle the word or phrase that completes each sentence.

1. Jhoon Rhee teaches _____.
   a. football   **b.** high jumps   **c.** tae kwon do

2. Rhee teaches people how to _____.
   a. keep their thoughts together
   b. jump higher than others
   c. go to school

3. Rhee was born in _____.
   a. the United States
   b. college
   c. Korea

4. Rhee first showed tae kwon do _____.
   a. to his friends
   b. during a college show
   c. during a college class

5. Rhee broke boards with his _____.
   a. hand   **b.** head   **c.** feet

6. During lessons, Rhee's students wear pads _____.
   a. when they hurt their hands
   b. to keep them safe
   c. when they break boards

Take Your Turn!
Why is Jim Trias called "the father of karate" in the United States? Research to find out.

The Drive to Win

Golf is a game played with golf clubs and a small ball. The ball has little round dents in it. The dents are called dimples. The clubs look like long sticks. There are many kinds of clubs. Some are called woods. These clubs have large heads. They are used to hit the ball far. Other clubs are called irons. They are all metal. The heads of these clubs are smaller and thin. They are used to hit the ball high in the air. Golfers carry bags that hold the clubs. There are 19 clubs to choose from. During important games, golfers can carry only 14 clubs in their bags.

Golfers play on a big golf course. Most golf courses have 18 holes. The holes are far apart. There are places with sand. There are places with water, too. The players do not want their balls to land in these places. They want to hit their balls on the green. The green is a place where the grass is short. The grass is always green here. The hole is always on the green. Flags on long sticks show where the hole is.

Golfers want to hit their balls into the holes. They do not want to use a lot of hits. Players count the number of hits it takes to get the ball into the hole. The best golfers can hit the ball two or three times on each hole. After all 18 holes are played, golfers add all the numbers together. This number is the score. Golfers want a low score. The golfer with the lowest score wins.

To begin play at each hole, the golfer puts the golf ball on a tee. A tee is a small stick made of wood. One end is sharp. The other end is flat. Golfers push the tee in the ground. They place their ball on the tee. Golfers hit the ball with a wood club. The first hit is called a drive. The other hits must be made where the ball stops. As the ball gets closer to the green, players do not hit the ball as hard. They use short, high hits. These hits are called chip shots. When the ball is on the green, golfers use a hit called a putt. The ball rolls on the ground. Hopefully, it will roll into the hole!

Go on to the next page.

The Drive to Win, p. 2

Circle the word that completes the analogy.

1. basketball : hoop   golf : _____
   a. flag   **b.** iron   **c.** hole

2. four : bases   _____ : holes
   a. nineteen   **b.** eighteen   **c.** fourteen

3. soccer : field   golf: _____
   a. green   **b.** sand   **c.** course

4. skis : poles   ball : _____
   a. clubs   **b.** hit   **c.** drive

5. fewest : points   _____ : score
   a. lowest   **b.** slowest   **c.** greatest

6. kick off : football   _____ : golf
   a. putt   **b.** chip   **c.** drive

Take Your Turn!

Find out what these words mean in a golf game: *par, birdie, eagle, bogey.*

There's a Tiger on the Course!

What did you do when you were six months old? Most children crawl. Others might begin to walk. But not Eldrick Woods. He watched his dad hit golf balls with a club. He tried to act like his dad! He began to swing his arms like he was playing golf, too. So, what happened to this child? He became a famous golfer at the age of 21. You have probably heard of him! His name is Tiger Woods.

Tiger was born on December 30, 1975. Tiger's dad gave him the nickname. "Tiger" was also the name of a good friend of Tiger's dad. Tiger began to play golf right away. He had his own set of small golf clubs. He played golf on the golf course with his dad. People began to watch Tiger Woods.

When Tiger was two years old, he was on a television show. He putted the ball with Bob Hope, a well-known TV star. By three years of age, Tiger was playing nine holes of golf. He made a score of 48. He averaged five hits of the ball for each hole! He was a star at the age of five. A golf magazine wrote a story about him. The magazine told the readers what a great golfer Tiger was.

Tiger loved to play golf. He won many tournaments. At the age of 21, he became a professional golfer. Now Tiger could get money when he won golf games. He was a great player. Tiger broke many records. In less than a year, he was the number-one golfer in the world. He won the Masters Tournament the same year. The Masters is a famous golf game. Tiger got the lowest score ever hit at this game. He was the youngest golfer to win, too. Tiger was also the first African American and Asian to win the Masters.

Tiger Woods keeps playing golf. He wins, too. But it is not really a surprise. Remember, he started playing when he was six months old. Maybe you should find out what you did at that age. You might find out that you could do something special, too.

Go on to the next page.

There's a Tiger on the Course!, p. 2

Complete the puzzle.

Across

2. At six _____ of age, Tiger swung his arms like he was playing golf.
3. When Tiger was _____, he played nine holes of golf.
5. A _____ golfer is someone who gets money when he or she wins a game.
6. Tiger made the _____ score in the Masters Tournament.

Down

1. The Masters Tournament is a famous golf _____.
2. Tiger was on _____ when he was two years old.
4. Someone who plays golf is a _____.

Take Your Turn!

What other games has Tiger Woods won?
Research to find out.

Dog-Gone Fun

Dear Diary,

I think my dogs are ready. They have worked hard. They are ready to pull the sled in the

dog-sled race next week. I have also worked hard. I have learned to be a musher. A musher is the person who drives the sled. A sled is made of wood. It has flat boards like skis. It glides over the snow. Some people think we are called mushers because we say "mush" to make the dogs go. That is not true. We say "All right!" or "Hike!" to make the dogs go.

My dogs are Alaskan Huskies. They have thick fur. Their fur keeps them warm when the temperature falls to 60° below zero Fahrenheit. They also have strong backs. They can pull big loads. Their feet have thick pads to keep them from getting cold. They like to work. To get them in shape, I take them for long runs. Sometimes they pull the sled. Sometimes they run without the sled. I lead them on ropes. I also am careful about what I feed the dogs. They must eat good food to help them stay strong.

The sled is about eight feet long. It weighs 40 pounds. There is a brake to help slow down the sled. A rope joins the dogs to the sled. The rope is called a gangline. The gangline has a harness for each dog. The harness is padded. The pads keep the dogs from being hurt.

My eight dogs and I will race in a long-distance race. This race will be about 150 miles. It will take several days. For all long races, I must pack an ax, a sleeping bag, and snowshoes. I also must pack two pounds of food for each dog for each day of the race. I will need food, too.

When we race, I stand on the back of the sled. I use my voice and words to tell the dogs how to run. The two dogs in the front are the lead dogs. When we go up a hill, I jump off the sled. I run beside it. Then the sled will not be as heavy. The dogs can pull it more easily. To win, I must have the fastest time. My dogs must be in good shape when I am done, too.

So, Diary, you see that I am ready for this race. Wish me luck!

Go on to the next page.

Dog-Gone Fun, p. 2

Circle the word that has the same or similar meaning to the word or words in bold type.

1. A **person who drives the sled** uses words to make the dogs go.
    a. cowboy   **b.** judge   **c.** musher

2. Alaskan Huskies have thick **hair** to keep them warm.
    a. fur   **b.** backs   **c.** ears

3. The dogs' feet have a thick **covering** to keep them from getting cold.
    a. pad   **b.** harness   **c.** fur

4. The harness is **covered with soft material.**
    a. cotton   **b.** padded   **c.** rope

5. In long races, a driver must pack a **bag to sleep in.**
    a. ax   **b.** sleeping bag   **c.** snowshoes

6. A driver stands on the **end** of the sled.
    a. back   **b.** harness   **c.** gangline

7. A driver **hops** off the sled to go up a hill.
    a. runs   **b.** slides   **c.** jumps

Take Your Turn!

What is the Iditarod Trail Dog Sled Race? How long is it? Where does it take place? Research to find out. Then make a map to show the trail.

It's a Dog's Life

Many people have dogs. They walk them. They play with them. They feed them. These are fun dogs. Some dogs work. A person who cannot see may have a dog. This dog helps the person walk along streets. The dog also helps the person find things around the house. Susan Butcher has some work dogs, too. She likes a sport that uses dogs. She is a musher. Susan drives a sled in dog-sled races.

Susan has raced in the hardest race. It is the Iditarod Trail Dog Sled Race. The race takes place in March. Drivers race from Anchorage to Nome, Alaska. They go over two mountains. The race course is over 1,100 miles long. It takes from ten days to three weeks for mushers to finish the race. The temperature can fall to 40° below zero. The wind can blow up to 140 miles per hour.

Susan has been in the race many times. She first raced in the Iditarod in 1978. She was the first woman to try this race. Many people said she would not finish the race. She did finish. She was the ninteenth person to cross the line. Each year she did better. Since then, Susan has won the race four times. Only one year did she have to quit. In 1985, her dog team was hurt by a wild moose. She could not race without her dogs.

Susan trains her dogs from the day they are born. She is the first person to hold the dogs. She is the first person to talk to the dogs. She loves them and plays with them. As the puppies grow, Susan takes them on long walks. They begin by going three miles. The dogs get their own house when they are one year old. She works with the dogs every day. She wants them to be strong. Soon she puts the dogs into a harness. They must get used to how it feels. Soon the dogs can run 25 miles each day.

Even though Susan's dogs are work dogs, she thinks of them as pets. She takes good care of them. Then, when Susan and her dog team are on the trail, the dogs take care of her.

Go on to the next page.

It's a Dog's Life, p. 2

Circle the word or phrase that completes each sentence.

1. Susan Butcher is a musher who _____.
   a. drives a dog sled in races
   b. mashes potatoes
   c. builds sleds

2. The Iditarod Trail Dog Sled Race is _____.
   a. over 1,100 miles long
   b. in Alaska
   c. both **a** and **b**

3. Susan was the first woman to _____.
   a. race in the Iditarod
   b. raise dogs to race
   c. win the Iditarod

4. She has won the Iditarod _____ times.
   a. four   **b.** nineteen   **c.** twenty-five

5. In one race, Susan had to stop because _____.
   a. her dog team was tired
   b. a moose hurt her dog team
   c. she got sick

6. Susan thinks of her dogs as _____.
   a. pets   **b.** children   **c.** workers

Take Your Turn!

The Iditarod Trail Dog Sled Race is for people who are older than 17. There is a shorter race for people under the age of 17. Find out how long the Jr. Iditarod Trail Dog Sled Race is.

Are You "Board"?

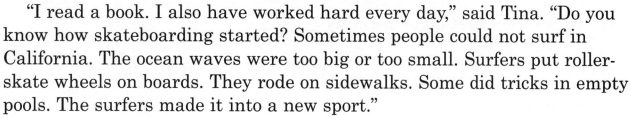

"Mark, let's go shred the sidewalk. I need to work on my ollies," said Tina.

"Tina, what did you just say?" asked Mark.

"Get with the skateboard talk, Mark. I know you just bought a skateboard. You also have a helmet and the pads to cover your arms, hands, and knees. They will keep you safe. Now you need to learn to skateboard," said Tina.

"How do you know so much?" asked Mark.

"I read a book. I also have worked hard every day," said Tina. "Do you know how skateboarding started? Sometimes people could not surf in California. The ocean waves were too big or too small. Surfers put roller-skate wheels on boards. They rode on sidewalks. Some did tricks in empty pools. The surfers made it into a new sport."

"Those boards must have been hard to ride," said Mark.

"They were not really safe, either. But someone had a new idea for wheels. They were softer. It was easier to ride on them. Now people have many choices when they buy skateboards. Wheels can be different sizes. Big wheels make the ride less bumpy. The board is called a deck. There are many kinds of decks. Some are short. Others are wide. It is important that a deck looks good. It should be painted with bright colors and many shapes. The last parts on the board are the trucks. They join the wheels to the deck," said Tina.

"Do you know about the kinds of skating?" asked Mark.

"There are two kinds. Vert is what many skaters do," answered Tina. "Here, people do tricks in a ramp. The ramps can look like half of a circle or just one quarter of a circle. The ramp is called a pipe. Skaters catch air to do a trick. It means they are in the air with the board. They can turn around or flip. In freestyle, skaters ride on sidewalks. They do ollies."

"There is that word again. What is an ollie?" asked Mark.

"It is a move where the rider is in the air. The feet are still on the board. Oh, there are some important rules to remember. Skaters should not ride in the road. Many parks have safe places for skaters to ride. Also, watch out for people walking. Now, are you ready to go shred some sidewalk?" asked Tina.

"If that means skate, yes! I need to work on my ollies!" laughed Mark.

Go on to the next page.

Are You "Board"?, p. 2

Use words from the Word List to complete the sentences.

Word List
wheels
pads
pipe
surfers
deck
pools
tricks
air

1. It is important to wear _____ to cover the arms, hands, and knees.

2. Skateboards were made by _____.

3. Tricks were first done in empty _____.

4. Big _____ make the ride on a skateboard less bumpy.

5. It is important that the _____ be painted bright colors.

6. A ramp is called a _____.

7. Vert is a kind of skateboarding where people do _____.

8. An ollie is a trick where the board and skater are in the _____.

Take Your Turn!

What are the names of some people who are known for skateboarding? Research on the Internet to find out.

Right on Target!

When you hear the name *Robin Hood*, what do you think about? Many people think about the story of Robin Hood. He used bows and arrows. Robin Hood was a hunter. Bows and arrows were one way for people during that time to get food.

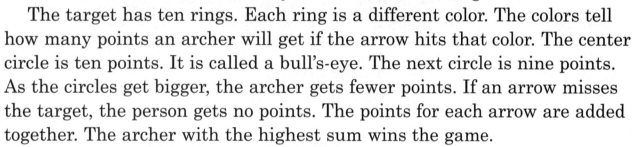

Now we can go to a food store to get food. There is no need for bows and arrows. However, some people still use them. They like to shoot arrows at a colorful circle for sport. This sport is called archery. The people in the sport are called archers. The circle they aim at is called a target.

The target has ten rings. Each ring is a different color. The colors tell how many points an archer will get if the arrow hits that color. The center circle is ten points. It is called a bull's-eye. The next circle is nine points. As the circles get bigger, the archer gets fewer points. If an arrow misses the target, the person gets no points. The points for each arrow are added together. The archer with the highest sum wins the game.

Different rules tell how many arrows an archer will shoot in a game. In some games, archers can have 36 arrows. In others, they may have only 12. To play a game, a line is drawn away from the target. Archers stand behind it. Archers take turns. They shoot three arrows each turn. The arrows have feathers on them. The feathers help the arrows fly straight. The arrow fits on the string of the bow. The string is pulled back by a finger. When the archer lets the string go, the arrow flies away. Some arrows can go 150 miles per hour.

It takes lots of practice to hit a target. The targets are small. Archers stand very far away. For example, think about a target that is 5 inches across. Now think about a football field. It is 100 yards long. When playing in big games, archers stand at one end of the field. They aim at the small target that is about 100 yards away.

In archery, the name *Robin Hood* has another meaning. In a well-known story, Robin Hood shot an arrow in the bull's-eye. He then shot another arrow. The point of the second arrow split the first arrow. When an archer talks about a Robin Hood, it means the archer did the same trick. If an archer can do that, he or she is as good as Robin Hood!

Go on to the next page.

Right on Target!, p. 2

Circle the word that has the same or similar meaning to the word or words in bold type.

1. Robin Hood used bows and arrows to get **something to eat**.
   a. food   **b.** water   **c.** circles

2. A **colorful circle** has ten rings.
   a. dish   **b.** pinwheel   **c.** target

3. Archers get **number scores** for hitting the target.
   a. points   **b.** padded   **c.** rope

4. Archers want to hit the **center circle**.
   a. target   **b.** bull's-eye   **c.** arrow

5. Feathers help the arrow to **move in the air** straight.
   a. fly   **b.** fall   **c.** grow

6. Archers can shoot three **sticks with points** each time.
   a. bows   **b.** arrows   **c.** targets

7. The archer with the highest **points added together** wins the game.
   a. sum   **b.** bull's-eye   **c.** game

Take Your Turn!

What is the highest score ever
recorded in an archery game?
Research to find out.

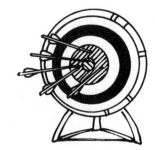

Put on Hold

What is wrestling?

Wrestling is a sport. Two people wrestle at a time. Wrestlers use their arms and legs to get the other person on the ground. Wrestlers need to have strong arms and legs. Yet they must be light on their feet. They need to move away quickly from the other person.

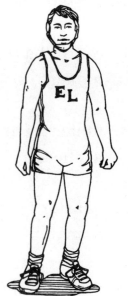

What equipment do wrestlers use?

Wrestlers work on mats. There is a large circle in the center. The circle marks the place to wrestle. The people wear clothing that is one piece. It is called a singlet. It fits close to the body. Wrestlers also wear shoes. The shoes are soft. They do not have heels. The shoes tie up to the ankles. Wrestles must wear something on their heads. It looks like a small helmet. It covers the head and ears. It has a strap under the chin.

What are the rules?

Wrestlers must weigh themselves. They wrestle in different weight groups, or classes. There are 10 to 13 different weight classes. Wrestlers work with people who are about their size. It makes the sport fair.

How is the sport done?

A match is a game between two wrestlers. A match has three rounds. Rounds can last two or three minutes. A referee is on the mat with the wrestlers. The referee makes sure the wrestlers follow the rules. The referee also gives points.

Wrestlers try to hold the other person down on the mat. They get points when they get a person down. Wrestlers can also score points when they get away. There are two ways to win a match. After three rounds, the wrestler with the most points wins. Another way to win is when one wrestler pins the other. A pin is where one wrestler's shoulders are flat on the mat. The wrestler holding the other down in a pin always wins.

Go on to the next page.

Put on Hold, p. 2

Circle the word that completes the analogy.

1. court : basketball   _____ : wrestling
   a. field   **b.** mat   **c.** class

2. uniform : baseball   _____ : wrestling
   a. shoes   **b.** helmet   **c.** singlet

3. quarter : game   round : _____
   a. match   **b.** class   **c.** circle

4. umpire : baseball player   _____ : wrestler
   a. goalie   **b.** referee   **c.** pitcher

5. _____ : rounds   nine : innings
   a. two   **b.** three   **c.** four

6. most : points   _____ : pin
   a. shoulders   **b.** knee   **c.** arm

Take Your Turn!

Sumo wrestling is a sport in Japan. How is it like the wrestling in the United States? How is it different? Research to find out.

Roping and Riding

Picture yourself sitting on a bull. It is snorting and stamping its feet. There is a rope tied around the bull. The rope is wrapped around your hand. It is the only thing that keeps you on the bull. The bull begins to move. It throws you to the sides of the chute. The chute is the small, wooden pen that leads out to the middle of the ring. You begin to wonder why you are a rodeo cowboy!

The chute opens. The bull jumps out. Its feet fly into the air. At the same time, you keep one hand up. Each time the bull jumps, you keep your heels on the bull. You get points for how much the bull jumps. You also get points for what you look like. In bull riding, you must stay on for eight seconds. You cannot fall off. Your free hand cannot touch yourself or the bull. If it does, you are out of the event.

Five, six, seven, eight! You made it. You jump off the bull. You race for the fence. You are safe. What you just did was a kind of event called rough stock riding. You also have to ride horses this way. In one event, you ride in a saddle. In the next event, you ride without a saddle. The rider with the most points wins.

There are other events for a rodeo rider. In those events, you race the clock. You win if you have the fastest time. Your favorite event is the steer event. You and your horse race beside a big steer. It weighs about 600 pounds. You grab its horns. You get it on the ground. The time stops when you have all of its feet facing the same way.

The other timed events are the steer roping, calf roping, team roping, and barrel racing. In steer roping, you ride after a steer. You throw a rope around its horns. The time stops when you have tied its back legs together. Calf roping is the same, but three legs are tied together. In the team roping, you work with another person to rope a steer. Barrel racing is fun, too. You race your horse around three barrels. You must be careful not to knock over a barrel. Five seconds will be added to your time for each barrel that goes down.

The work is hard. You could get hurt. But it is fun! You know that all the animals are safe, too. There are rules that make sure the animals are not hurt. A veterinarian looks at them many times.

You hear your name called. It is time to get ready for the next event.

Go on to the next page.

Roping and Riding, p. 2

Circle the word or phrase that completes each sentence.

1. In bull riding, you must _____.
   a. stay on for eight seconds
   b. hold onto the saddle
   c. tie together the feet of the bull

2. In the rough stock riding events, the winner _____.
   a. gets the best time
   b. looks the best
   c. gets the most points

3. In steer roping, you must tie _____ legs together.
   a. two
   b. three
   c. four

4. In calf roping, the time stops when _____.
   a. the two back feet are tied
   b. three feet are tied
   c. all four feet face the same way

5. The person with the fastest time wins in _____.
   a. barrel racing
   b. bull riding
   c. bronco riding

6. A _____ looks at the animals to make sure they are not hurt.
   a. cowboy   **b.** veterinarian   **c.** referee

Take Your Turn!

Rodeo clowns are often seen at rodeos. What do they do? How do they help the riders? Research to find out.

Striking It Rich

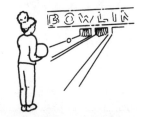

Dear Carl,

   I went bowling today. It was so much fun! Aunt Diane was a great teacher. When I first went into the bowling alley, I was not sure I could play the game. The bowling balls looked heavy. They weigh from 6 to 16 pounds. Aunt Diane gave me a ball that was only seven pounds. She showed me how to put my fingers into the three holes.

   Bowling is played on a lane, or alley. An alley is a long wooden path that looks like a straight road. To play the game, you roll the bowling ball down the alley. There is a line at one end of the alley. You cannot cross it or touch it with your foot. You cannot get points if you do.

   There are ten pins at the other end of the lane. They look like bottles. They are set in a triangle. You get two rolls to knock down all ten pins. I did not do well at first. My balls went into the gutter. The gutter runs beside the alley. It is lower than the alley. It looks like the gutter beside a road. You do not get any points when the ball lands in the gutter.

   Aunt Diane said bowlers take turns. They play ten times. Each turn is called a frame. Aunt Diane made three strikes. A strike is when a bowler knocks down all ten pins with the first ball. She got ten points for each strike. Aunt Diane also made two spares. A spare is when a bowler knocks down all ten pins with two rolls. She got ten points for each spare, too. Since I kept rolling my ball in the gutter, I got many errors. An error is when you do not get any points. However, one time I did knock six pins over. Then I got six points. After all ten frames have been played, the bowler with the highest score wins. I guess you know that Aunt Diane won.

   Aunt Diane said we could go again tomorrow. I should do much better. Who knows! Maybe I will make a strike!
Your friend,
Sonya

Go on to the next page.

Striking It Rich, p. 2

✎ **Write** the word that completes each sentence.

1. An _____ looks like a straight wooden road.

2. A _____ looks like a bottle.

3. A _____ is like an inning in baseball.

4. A gutter of an alley looks like the gutter beside a

_____.

Answer the question.

5. A bowling ball weighs from 6 to 16 pounds. Look around the school or
   your house. Look for items that have weights written on them. List
   the things you find and their weights. How many of those items do
   you need to equal the weight of a bowling ball?

   _____

   _____

   _____

   _____

   _____

Take Your Turn!

The highest score a bowler can make is 300. A bowler
must roll all strikes to do so. Very few people have
bowled all strikes. Research to find the names of
several people who have scored 300 points.

UNIT 3: Teaming Up

The Goal Is the Game

Football is a game that started in the United States. Players run, pass, or kick an oval ball. It is called a football. The football is about 11 inches long. The game is played on a field that is 100 yards long. The last line on each end is the goal line. Teams try to get the ball across these lines. Teams score points if they do. There are also goalposts behind the goal lines. These posts have two arms high in the air. Kicking the ball through the arms will give a team points, too.

Two teams play the game. Each team is given a goal line. They want to keep the other team from getting to this line. When a player crosses the goal line, the team gets six points. It is called a touchdown. That team also gets a turn to kick the ball. They will get another point if the ball goes between the arms of the goalpost. The team with the most points at the end of the game wins.

Each team can only have 11 players on the field. Each player has a special job. Some players throw the ball. Other players kick the ball. Some players keep the other team from getting near the ball. They try to block people. They also try to tackle the player who has the ball. A tackle is when a player pulls someone down on the ground.

Football is a rough game. People can get hurt. Players wear special pads to keep them safe. They wear big helmets on their heads. They also wear a mouthpiece. It is plastic. It protects their teeth and tongue.

A game is divided into four parts, called quarters. Each quarter lasts 15 minutes. A team gets four tries to move the ball. They must pass or run the ball ten yards. If they go ten yards, they get four more tries. If they cannot move the ball, the other team gets a turn.

Many people help the football teams. There are several coaches. The coaches tell the players what to do. They also decide who plays in the game. Referees are on the field with the players. They wear white and black striped clothes. They make sure that the players follow the rules.

The people watching the game are important, too. They are the fans. They cheer for their favorite team. It helps the players want to win. If you ever go to a game, be sure to yell. It might help your favorite team to win!

Go on to the next page.

The Goal Is the Game, p. 2

Use words from the Word List to complete the sentences.

1. There are _____ players on each team.

2. Players run, pass, and _____ the ball.

3. A _____ tells the team what to do.

4. A _____ makes sure the players follow

    the rules.

5. A _____ is when a player pulls

    someone down on the ground.

6. A team gets _____ tries to move the ball.

7. Players wear _____ to stay safe.

8. The team with the most _____ at the end of the game

    wins.

Word List
points
eleven
referee
four
kick
pads
coach
tackle

Take Your Turn!

What is the Super Bowl? When was the
first Super Bowl played? Who won that
first game? Research to find out.

Nothing But a Bronco

"The Broncos have won! The Denver Broncos have won the 1997 Super Bowl game! Led by John Elway, the Broncos have won the biggest football game of the year!"

That news came over the radio. Finally, after 15 years, John Elway had his Super Bowl ring. John had worked hard. He was the quarterback. John called the plays. He threw the football, or he passed it to someone on the team to run. He had been with the Denver Broncos football team for 15 years. John had been to the Super Bowl three other times. But this was his first win.

John made football history. He became known as the "winningest" quarterback. He broke many passing records. He also broke many touchdown records.

People on the Broncos team began calling John "The Arm." When he was a boy, John loved to throw things. He would practice throwing rocks at bottles. He also would throw all kinds of balls. The practice paid off. He could throw well. He became a sports star in high school. John was good at football, basketball, and baseball. Many colleges wanted John to come to their school. Over 60 colleges asked him to play on their teams.

John chose Stanford University. He played both football and baseball at Stanford. He set many passing records on the football team. People began to watch John Elway. They called him one of the best quarterbacks ever to play in college. His record as a baseball player was good, too. John was a pitcher. He would throw the ball to the batters. He once threw a ball that went 92 miles per hour.

John decided to play football after college. In 1983 he joined the Denver Broncos. He quickly became the starting quarterback. And the rest of the story is now Super Bowl history!

Go on to the next page.

Nothing But a Bronco, p. 2

Complete the puzzle.

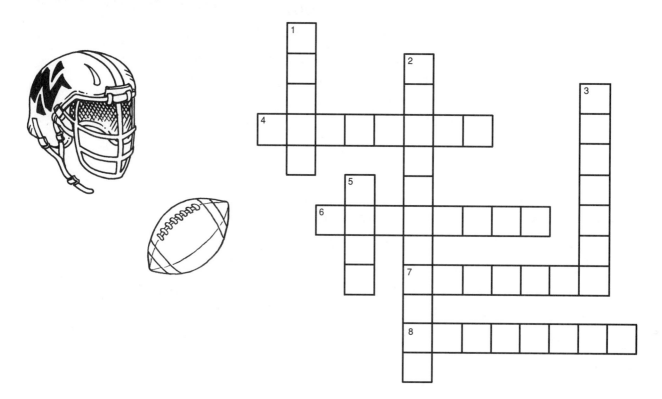

Across

4. John Elway played _____ when he got out of college.
6. John was a _____ pitcher in college, too.
7. When he was a boy, John threw rocks at _____.
8. Sixty _____ wanted John to come to their school.

Down

1. John could _____ well because he practiced hard.
2. John is known as the "winningest" _____.
3. He plays for a team called the Denver _____.
5. The Super Bowl is the biggest football _____.

Take Your Turn!

Which teams have won the Super Bowl for the last five years? Research
to find out.

You Can Dribble Here!

Basketball is a favorite game. People can play it inside or outside. All the players need are a basketball and a goal. A basketball is orange and round. It is made of rubber. The basketball goal has three parts. One part is a round circle of metal. This circle is called a hoop. A net is on the bottom of the hoop. The hoop joins the backboard. The backboard is a piece of wood or plastic shaped like a rectangle. Players try to shoot the basketball through the hoop. The ball can bounce against the backboard. It helps the ball go through the hoop.

Most basketball games are played on a court. The court is shaped like a rectangle. It is large area made of wood. There is a goal at each end. Players run up and down the court. They bounce the basketball as they run. Bouncing the ball is called dribbling. Players can also pass the ball to each other.

Two teams play the game. Each team is given a goal. Teams try to get the ball through the hoop. They score points if they do. Players can score one, two, or three points. Teams also try to keep each other from scoring points. The team with the most points at the end of the game wins.

Each team can only have five players on the court. Some players are good at shooting the ball when they are far away from the goal. Others are good at keeping the other team from making baskets. They all must be good runners. They must also be good shooters when they are close to the basket.

Each team tries to get the ball. They want to make a basket. If the ball goes outside the court, the team who did not touch the ball last will get it. Also, if a player shoots the ball at a basket and misses, anyone can get the ball. Players jump high to get the ball. Here is a list of other ways the ball goes to the other team:

★ a team scores some points.

★ a player touches someone who is shooting the ball.

★ a team breaks the rules.

★ a player takes the ball as it is being passed.

People do not need two goals to play basketball. They can play using one goal. The players still make two teams. But, both teams shoot at the same goal. It is just as much fun as playing on a court, and players do not have to run as much!

Go on to the next page.

You Can Dribble Here!, p. 2

Circle the word that has the same or similar meaning to the word or words in bold type.

1. In basketball, the goal is made from a **circle of metal**, a net, and a backboard.
   a. ring   **b.** bucket   **c.** hoop

2. Players play on a **large rectangular area made of wood**.
   a. field   **b.** court   **c.** shelf

3. To move the ball, players **bounce the ball up and down**.
   a. dribble   **b.** pass   **c.** shoot

4. Players get points when the **orange round sphere** falls through the hoop.
   a. baseball   **b.** basketball   **c.** football

5. Each **basketball group** can have five players on the court.
   a. team   **b.** fan   **c.** family

6. All basketball players are good at **putting one foot in front of the other very fast**.
   a. walking   **b.** running   **c.** jumping

7. The other team gets the ball if a player **does not follow** the rules.
   a. breaks   **b.** yells   **c.** lists

Take Your Turn!

Find the names of three professional basketball teams. Who plays on these teams? Write the name of one player from each team.

Super Fun—Super Star

Who plays basketball with cartoon characters? Who talks about tennis shoes on television? Who is the greatest basketball player in history? You guessed it! That person is Michael Jordan!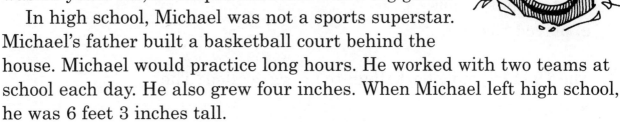

When he was young, Michael liked all sports. However, Michael's favorite sport was baseball. He played on a team. He was a pitcher. When Michael was 12 years old, he helped his team win a big game.

In high school, Michael was not a sports superstar. Michael's father built a basketball court behind the house. Michael would practice long hours. He worked with two teams at school each day. He also grew four inches. When Michael left high school, he was 6 feet 3 inches tall.

Many colleges wanted Michael to be on their teams. He chose the University of North Carolina. He became a starter his first year there. Michael helped his team make it to the championship game that same year. Michael made the winning basket. He was 17 feet away. People began to watch Michael play.

In 1984, Michael went to the Olympics. He played on the United States basketball team. The team was called "The Dream Team." Many well-known basketball players were on this team. They won the gold medal.

Michael became a professional basketball player after his third year in college. He was chosen by the Chicago Bulls. He wore the number 23. Michael chose that number because of his older brother, Larry. His brother played basketball, too. The brother wore the number 45. Michael wanted 23. It was about half of the number Larry wore. Michael wanted that number because he hoped that he could play half as well as his brother. Michael also wore his Carolina blue shorts under his Chicago Bulls shorts. He said it gave him luck. In one game, Michael broke a record. He made 63 points in one game.

Michael's father was killed in 1993. Michael stopped playing basketball. He tried to play baseball. But, his love of basketball was great. Two years later, Michael began to play basketball again. He returned to the Bulls. He helped his team get to the playoffs. Everybody thought Michael was super—and a star!

Go on to the next page.

Super Fun—Super Star, p. 2

Circle the word or phrase that completes each sentence.

1. Michael Jordan played _____ when he was 12.
   a. basketball   **b.** baseball   **c.** soccer

2. At the University of North Carolina, Michael _____.
   a. made the winning basket in a championship game
   b. grew four inches
   c. played baseball

3. The 1984 Olympic basketball team was called "The _____."
   a. Super Five
   b. Dream Team
   c. Court Kings

4. Michael played for the _____ after college.
   a. San Antonio Spurs
   b. Carolina Tarheels
   c. Chicago Bulls

5. Michael wore number 23 because it was _____.
   a. the only number left
   b. his lucky number
   c. about half the number that his brother wore

6. For luck during games, Michael wore _____.
   a. a gold necklace
   b. his Carolina blue shorts
   c. blue socks

Take Your Turn!

What is the average number of points
that Michael Jordan has scored in
each game? Use the Internet to help you.

This Game Is a Hit!

You are in a baseball championship! You are the pitcher for your team. There are players on all three bases. Your team is ahead by one run. It is the last inning. You must get the next batter out. If you do, your team can win the game!

Baseball is a favorite game for all ages. A baseball field has three bases and a home plate. The field looks like a diamond. To play, you only need a baseball, bat, glove, and base markers. Two teams play the game. Teams have nine players. One team bats, and the other team plays in the field. The team in the field tries to catch the ball and get the batting team out. The batting team tries to hit the ball and run to all the bases. A batting team has three outs. The teams trade places after three outs. The team with the most points at the end of the game wins.

You think about how to throw the ball. You want to throw three strikes. A strike is when the batter swings the bat and misses the ball or the ball is hit outside the foul line. You must make sure the ball flies over home plate. If it does not, the pitch is a ball. Four balls mean that the batter goes to first base.

You pitch the ball. "STRIKE 1!" the umpire yells.

Even if the batter hits the ball, the players in the field will help. They can get an out in three ways. One way is that the ball gets to first base before the batter. Also, someone on your team can catch a "fly" ball hit high into the air before it hits the ground. Finally, someone on your team can tag any base runner with the ball.

You pitch the ball again. "STRIKE 2!" the umpire yells.

There are other rules in baseball. Once on base, the runner can only go after a teammate hits the ball. Also, the runner must go to the next base if a teammate is on the base behind. However, if there is no one on that base, the runner doesn't have to run. When a teammate hits a fly ball, the runner must stay on base until the ball hits the ground or someone on your team catches it. Then the runner can run to as many bases as possible without being tagged by the ball. As runners pass each base, they must touch it with their foot. Runners score a run when they touch home plate.

Here is your next pitch. Can you get the last out? "STRIKE 3!" the umpire yells. You did it! Your team won the championship game!

Go on to the next page.

This Game Is a Hit!, p. 2

Circle the word or phrase that completes each sentence.

1. There are _____ players on a baseball team.
   a. three   **b.** nine   **c.** twelve

2. Each team gets three _____ before the teams change places.
   a. outs   **b.** strikes   **c.** runs

3. A runner may not go to the next base until _____.
   a. the ball is hit
   b. the batter is out
   c. the pitcher throws the ball

4. A strike is when _____.
   a. the batter hits the ball
   b. the batter swings and misses the ball
   c. a runner touches home plate

5. The team in the field tries to _____.
   a. hit the ball
   b. get the hitting team out
   c. run the bases

6. A player is out when he or she _____.
   a. is tagged by the ball
   b. hits a ball past the foul line
   c. touches first base

Take Your Turn!

What is the World Series? Which teams have won it for the last five years? Research to find out.

Baseball's Babe

Who was Babe Ruth?

Babe Ruth played baseball. His real name was George Herman Ruth. He was born in 1895. He got his name "Babe" when he first started playing professional baseball. He was 19 years old. The players on his team said he was very young. They said he was just a babe.

When did Babe begin baseball?

As a child, Babe Ruth did not always behave. His parents sent him to a different school. They hoped he would learn to act better. A priest at the school liked Babe. He wanted to help the boy. The priest worked with Babe. He taught Babe how to hit and pitch. Baseball gave Babe something to think about. He played on several school teams. He played with students who were older. Babe stayed at the school until he was 18. Then he went to play ball for a minor-league team. He was their pitcher. This team helped him work hard. They taught Babe more about playing baseball.

What did Babe do?

At the age of 20, Babe joined the Red Sox. It was a major-league team. He was a good pitcher. Babe helped the team win many games. But Babe was also a good batter. If he did not pitch a game, Babe played first base in the field. He made history. He broke many records. The biggest news happened when Babe hit 29 home runs in one year. The Red Sox went to the World Series two times.

Babe changed teams. He then played for the New York Yankees. He kept hitting well. People called him the "Sultan of Swat." Many people came to watch Babe play. The team needed a bigger place for their games. The people who owned the team built a new baseball field. The building would seat 60,000 people. The seats were always full. Babe hit 60 home runs in one year, breaking his old record of 29 home runs. He also helped the Yankees make it to seven World Series. He played for the Yankees until 1934.

One year later, Babe stopped playing baseball. In his baseball career, he hit 729 home runs. His batting average was .342. As a pitcher, he had 97 wins and 46 losses. He was one of the first players to become a member of the Baseball Hall of Fame.

Go on to the next page.

Baseball's Babe, p. 2

Use words from the Word List to complete the sentences.

Word List

pitcher
Swat
young
priest
batter
seven
behave
Fame

1. Babe Ruth got his name because he was so

   _____.

2. As a child, Babe did not always _____.

3. A _____ taught Babe how to hit and

   pitch.

4. Babe became a _____ for the Red Sox.

5. He hit lots of home runs because he was a good _____.

6. Babe helped the Yankees go to _____ World Series.

7. People called Babe the "Sultan of _____."

8. He was one of the first players to get into the Baseball Hall of

   _____.

Take Your Turn!

Which players now hold the records for most home
runs in a season, best batting average for a season,
and most visits to the World Series?

That's Using Your Head!

Dear Emily,

I am learning to play soccer. I am on a team called the Panthers. We run up and down the field. We kick a ball with our feet. It is called dribbling. The ball looks like a black and white checkerboard. The field is a large, green rectangle. There is a goal on each end of the field. The goal is a large net that looks like an open box. In a soccer game, we try to kick the ball into the net. We score points if we do. It is called a goal. In a game, the team with the most goals wins.

There are 15 people on my team. In a game, though, only 11 players are on the field at a time. In soccer, you cannot touch the ball with your hands. You can only use your feet and your head. I don't like to use my head, though. It hurts! Only one player can touch the ball. This person is called a goalie. The goalie stands in front of the goal. The goalie tries to keep the ball from going into the net.

We wear uniforms. Our uniforms are black and yellow. The goalie always wears a big shirt. It helps the referee know who can touch the ball. We also wear shin guards. These are pads that cover a player's lower legs. Sometimes I get kicked in the leg. It doesn't hurt, though. The shin guards keep me safe.

The coach said that the game has two parts, called halves. Basketball has parts called halves, too. Each half is 45 minutes long. I am glad we have extra players. The coach said that we can come out of the game if we get tired. She will let another player take our place.

Our first game is Saturday. I hope that you will come watch me play. Maybe I will score a goal.

Sincerely,
Rita

Go on to the next page.

That's Using Your Head!, p. 2

✎ **Write** the word that completes each sentence.

1. A soccer _____ looks like a black and white checkerboard.

2. A _____ looks like a large, green rectangle.

3. A _____ is large net that looks like an open box.

4. Soccer is played in halves like _____.

Answer the question.

5. How is soccer the same as basketball? How is it different?

_____

_____

_____

_____

_____

Take Your Turn!

What are some names of professional soccer teams? Who are some people who play on these teams? Research to find out.

Pelé Has a Ball!

"Okay, Cosmos, we have a game tomorrow. We need to play our best. We need to live up to our team name," said Coach Allan.

"What do you mean? What does our team name mean?" asked Sandy.

"Pelé was a famous soccer player. He played on a team called the Cosmos. They won many games," answered the coach.

"What did he do? Tell us about him," said Samantha.

"Pelé was born in Brazil. His father was a soccer player. Pelé's dad got hurt. He could not play any more. The family was poor. Pelé and his friends played soccer in the street. For a ball, they filled a big sock with paper. They tied string around the sock to make it round. They would kick the sock. Pelé's dad showed him how to play better. His father would be the goalie. Pelé would run and dribble the ball. He would try to score a goal. Sometimes he would get the ball past his dad."

"I bet that was hard to do if his dad played soccer," said Samantha.

"It was," said Coach Allan, "but Pelé worked hard. He and his friends decided to start a soccer team. Pelé was very good. At the age of 11, he got to play on a city team. He led the team to a big game win. At 17, he became a professional soccer player. He played for a team called the Santos. He helped the team win the World Cup Championship. It is a big game for professional soccer players. It was the first time that Brazil had won the game. Pelé played with the Santos for 18 years. Everybody liked Pelé. He was kind and a super soccer player. Then he quit playing soccer."

"Coach, you said that Pelé's team name was the same as ours."

"Well, Pelé came back to play soccer one year later. Some people in the United States wanted him to play again. He left Brazil. He played on a team called the Cosmos. He was 37 years old. He helped the Cosmos win a game called the Soccer Bowl. Pelé decided to stop playing soccer again. For his last game, the Santos, his old team, were asked to play the Cosmos. In the game, Pelé played half of the game with the Cosmos and the other half with the Santos!" said Coach Allan.

"Well, Coach, we will try to run and be good sports like Pelé. But I think we should use a soccer ball instead of a sock filled with paper," said Samantha.

Go on to the next page.

Pelé Has a Ball!, p. 2

Circle the word or phrase that completes each sentence.

1. Pelé played _____.
   a. soccer   **b.** football   **c.** basketball

2. He was born in _____.
   a. New York   **b.** Mexico   **c.** Brazil

3. Pelé and his friends made a ball by filling _____.
   a. a sock with paper
   b. a balloon with air
   c. a shirt with grass

4. Pelé learned to play the game _____.
   a. from his friends
   b. on a team
   c. from his dad

5. At 17, Pelé played _____.
   a. for a city team
   b. on a team called the Santos
   c. in the United States

6. Pelé went to the United States to _____.
   a. play for a team called the Cosmos
   b. teach other teams how to play
   c. take a vacation

Take Your Turn!

How many goals did Pelé make during his career as a professional player? Research to find out.

This Game Is Cool!

Ice hockey is a game played on ice. Players wear skates. They use sticks and a small rubber circle that looks like a hamburger bun. This circle is called a puck. The sticks are bent at one end. Players use the sticks to slide the puck across the ice.

Players wear many pads to cover their bodies. They wear a helmet, too. The puck can fly up. It could hurt players if they were not covered. Players also wear mouthpieces to protect their teeth and tongue.

Hockey players play on an oval rink. The lines on the ice mark the playing area. There is a net on each end of the rink. The nets are called goals. Each team is given a goal. They want to keep the other team from getting the puck in their goal. Teams score a point if the puck goes in. The team with the most points at the end of the game wins. The rink also has a wall around it. The top part of the wall is clear plastic. It keeps the people watching the game safe from a flying puck.

Two teams play the game. There are six skaters from each team on the ice. One player is the goalie. The goalie stays in front of the goal. To begin play, two skaters stand in the middle of the rink. A referee drops the puck between the players. The players try to get the puck. They pass it to a teammate with their stick. The puck must always be moving. Even if the puck goes outside the lines of the rink, players must get it as it slides back inside the lines.

Ice hockey can be rough. The rules tell who can shoot the puck. The rules also tell when people can bump into each other. Referees stay on the ice. They watch the skaters carefully. When players break the rules, it is called a penalty. They must sit in a small room beside the rink called a penalty box. Their team will play with only five players. It is a good time for the other team. They have a better chance to score when a player is missing from the other team.

A game is divided into three parts, called periods. Each period is 20 minutes long. Hockey can be played inside in a building or outside in very cold weather. However, many people like to play hockey for fun—especially during the summer. It is a cool place to hang out when it is hot outside.

Go on to the next page.

This Game Is Cool, p. 2

Circle the word or words that complete the analogy.

1. court : basketball   rink : _____
   a. kickball   **b.** soccer   **c.** ice hockey

2. baseball : bat   _____ : stick
   a. puck   **b.** skates   **c.** pads

3. 15 : quarter   20 : _____
   a. match   **b.** period   **c.** half

4. umpire : baseball player   _____ : skater
   a. goalie   **b.** referee   **c.** pitcher

5. foul : basketball   _____ : ice hockey
   a. rules   **b.** penalty   **c.** box

6. basketball : _____   puck : slide
   a. dribble   **b.** kick   **c.** carry

Take Your Turn!

How is hockey like soccer? How is it
different? Write a paragraph to compare the
two games.

Skating to the Great One

Wayne Gretzky was almost three. The Gretzky family lived in Canada. It was winter. The stream was finally frozen. Wayne's father took him out to ice-skate for the first time. His father had also made a little hockey stick for him. Wayne swung the stick. He fell several times. His father began to teach Wayne how to play hockey. Wayne loved to skate and play with the stick. His grandmother helped him, too. Wayne made his first goal with her. He shot a softball through her legs.

Wayne's dad made an ice rink in the backyard. Wayne skated around cans. He jumped over sticks. He practiced all the time. When Wayne was six years old, he joined a team. He played with boys who were older. Wayne wanted to wear number 99. His favorite hockey star was Gordie Howe. Gordie wore number 9. Gordie had the record for the most points ever scored in hockey history. Wayne wanted to be as good as Gordie. Wayne made 27 goals his first year.

Wayne kept working hard. He was not a fast skater. But Wayne was a smart skater. He could move around other players quickly. By the age of 14, he had made almost 1,000 goals. Hockey was too easy for Wayne!

By the age of 17, Wayne became a professional hockey player. He joined the Edmonton Oilers in Canada. He helped his team win many games. He was kind to everyone. Wayne let people know that the whole team worked together to win. People began to call him "The Great One."

In 1988, Wayne joined a new team. The team was called the Los Angeles Kings. Wayne helped the team to win the biggest hockey game of the year several times. He also broke many of Gordie Howe's records. Gordie Howe was there each time to watch.

To date, Wayne holds the record for the most goals, most assists, and most points for a season. He also holds the same records in hockey history. In 1998, *The Hockey News* magazine voted Wayne as the top hockey player in history. Now that is a great one!

Go on to the next page.

Skating to the Great One, p. 2

Circle the word or phrase that completes each sentence.

1. Wayne Gretzky went ice-skating for the first time when he was almost _____.

   a. two   **b.** three   **c.** six

2. Wayne made his first goal by shooting a ball _____.
   a. through his grandmother's legs
   b. past his father
   c. through the trunks of two trees

3. Wayne's favorite hockey star was _____.
   a. Michael Jordan
   b. Gordie Howe
   c. Edmonton Oilers

4. People began to call Wayne _____.
   a. Los Angeles King
   b. Super Skater
   c. The Great One

5. Wayne let people know that the team _____.
   a. was mean to him
   b. worked together to win
   c. was better than any other

6. In 1998, a magazine voted Wayne as the _____ in history.
   a. top hockey player
   b. nicest hockey player
   c. hockey player with the most points

Take Your Turn!

Wayne joined a new hockey team in 1997. What team did he join?
Research to find out.

Get Set for This Game

What is volleyball?

Volleyball is a game. Two teams play on a court. There is a tall net in the middle of the court. There are six people on each team. Players hit a ball across a net. They use their hands. The ball cannot touch the floor.

What equipment do players need?

The game is played with a net and a ball. The net is only three feet wide, but it is over seven feet off the ground. The ball is made of white leather. It weighs less than a pound. Players may wear knee pads. Sometimes they dive on the ground for a ball. The knee pads keep their knees from being hurt.

What are the rules?

Players use their hands to hit the ball over the net. Hands may be open, closed, or together. A team has three chances to hit the ball. Play will stop if the following rules are broken:
★ a player throws, catches, or lifts the ball.
★ a player hits the ball two times in a row.
★ the ball lands outside the court line.
★ the ball hits the floor.
A referee watches the game. If any of these rules are broken, the game stops. The other team will get a turn to serve the ball.

How is volleyball played?

A player stands behind the court to serve. The ball is hit over the net. The other team tries to hit it back. Since the team has three chances to hit the ball, the team uses the pattern "bump, set, spike." A bump is when a person hits the ball straight into the air. This player's hands are together. A set is when a second player uses the fingers to push the ball into the air. The ball moves close to the net. A spike is when another player jumps into the air. With one hand, the person will hit the ball over the net. Players will keep hitting the ball back and forth until the referee sees that a rule is broken. Teams score points only when they serve. They play to 15 points. That makes one match. A team must win two out of three matches to win the game.

Go on to the next page.

87

Get Set for This Game, p. 2

Circle the word that has the same or similar meaning to the word or words in bold type.

1. Volleyball players use **parts of their body with fingers** to get the ball over the net.
   a. feet   **b.** hands   **c.** heads

2. Players may wear **fabric coverings** on their knees.
   a. shirts   **b.** shoes   **c.** pads

3. A team has three **turns** to hit the ball over the net.
   a. chances   **b.** jumps   **c.** serves

4. Play stops if the ball touches the **ground.**
   a. floor   **b.** net   **c.** line

5. Teams score points only if they **put the ball into play.**
   a. spike   **b.** hit   **c.** serve

6. In a bump, a player's hands are **side by side.**
   a. together   **b.** apart   **c.** open

7. Teams use the pattern of bump, set, **hit the ball with one hand over the net.**
   a. serve   **b.** slap   **c.** spike

Take Your Turn!

What years did the United States win the gold medal in men's volleyball in the Olympic games? Research to find out.

Sled and Slide

Have you ever raced down a snowy hill on a sled? What did it feel like? Some people like sledding so much that they do a sport called luge. *Luge* is a French word that means "sled." One or two people can do the luge. The people who ride a luge are called sliders.

A luge sled has two runners. The runners are the parts of the sled that touch the snow. They are curved at the front. They look a little like the runners on the sled you ride. There are blades on the bottom of the runners. They are smooth. The blades help the sled glide over ice. The luge does not have brakes.

When people ride on a luge, they lie down. Their bodies face up. Their feet are at the front of the luge. Their heads and feet hang off. When two sliders ride at the same time, they must work together. The first person must watch where the luge goes. That person moves the runners of the luge with the knees. The back slider helps to start the sled. Otherwise, that person stays very still. Any small move could cause the luge to slide. The sliders could be hurt.

The luge track is built on a side of a mountain. The track looks like half of a tube. The track is covered with ice. The top part of the track is straight. It helps the sliders to go fast. The bottom part has lots of turns and loops.

Pairs of sliders go very fast. The sleds can go over 80 miles per hour. The speed makes their heads pull down. Sliders wear a neck strap. The neck strap is a piece of fabric they wear under their suits. It holds their heads up so they will not fall on the ice.

Sliders wear suits and gloves that fit close to the body. The gloves have small spikes on the knuckles. They wear soft shoes that are smooth on the bottoms. They also wear a helmet. The helmet has a cover on it that fits over the face. It keeps the face safe if they fall off the sled.

To get the sled started, the sliders sit on the luge. They hold onto handles at the beginning of the course. They rock the sled back and forth. Then they use their knuckles to push themselves forward. Both sliders quickly lie down. They are off! They twist and turn—slide and glide. The fastest time wins.

Go on to the next page.

Sled and Slide, p. 2

Across

2. *Luge* is a French word that means _____.
4. The _____ are the parts of the sled that touch the snow.
6. A luge track is covered with _____.
7. A person moves the runners of the sled with the _____.

Down

1. The _____ have spikes on them.
3. The bottom part of a track has lots of _____ and loops.
5. A person who rides a luge is called a _____.

Take Your Turn!

What is the history of the luge? Research on the Internet to find out.

Fast Feet—Fast Ball

Lacrosse is the oldest game in the United States. Native Americans played it. Sometimes the game was fun. Many times the game was played if two tribes did not agree. The tribes made goals. They used sticks and a ball. The players tried to get the ball into the other tribe's goal. The games were rough. The tribe that won the game also won the argument.

Players still use a stick and ball. The sticks look the same. The sticks are three to six feet long. There is a loop on the end. The loop has a net in it. The ball is small and hard. It is smaller than a baseball. Players run with the ball in their nets. They throw it to their teammates. They run fast. The ball moves fast. It can fly 100 miles per hour.

Players wear a helmet. The helmet has bars across the front. Players also wear pads under their shirts. Big gloves cover their hands, too. Players do not wear anything on their legs. Men wear shorts. Girls wear skirts with shorts under them. They can run better this way.

In lacrosse, each team has a goal. A goalie stands in front. As in soccer, the goalie is the only player who can touch the ball. The other players run with the ball. They throw it to each other. They try to make a goal. The other team tries to take the ball away. A referee watches the teams play. Players can bump the person who has the ball. This move is called a check. However, players cannot use their sticks to trip or hit another player. If a player breaks the rules, the referee tells that person to sit out for several minutes. The other team has a good chance to make a point since the team has one fewer person on the field. Each goal gives the team one point. The team with the most points wins.

Go on to the next page.

Name _____ Date _____

Fast Feet—Fast Ball, p. 2

Circle the word or phrase that completes each sentence.

1. Lacrosse was first played by _____.
   a. college players
   b. Native Americans
   c. soccer players

2. There is a hoop and _____ on the end of a lacrosse stick.
   a. net   **b.** ball   **c.** bars

3. Lacrosse players do not wear anything on their legs because _____.
   a. they get hot
   b. it is against the rules
   c. they can run better

4. The goalie is the only player who can _____.
   a. touch the ball
   b. throw the ball
   c. run with the ball

5. A check is when _____.
   a. a player bumps into another person
   b. the goalie catches the ball
   c. when a player makes a goal

6. A person who breaks a rule must _____.
   a. leave the game
   b. sit out for several minutes
   c. give the ball to the referee

Take Your Turn!

How is lacrosse like ice hockey? How is it different? Write a paragraph that compares the two games.

Pony Play: Polo

You are on a horse. You are looking around the field. There are four people on each team. They all ride horses. There are three other people on horses, too. They are the umpire and the referees. They make sure that people play by the rules. Veterinarians are nearby. Veterinarians are animal doctors. They make sure the horses stay safe. They look at the horses before and after the game.

The field is very big. It is the largest area for any ball game. You need the space for the horses to run safely. Also, you must remember the history of the game. At one time, people had 200 horses and players on a field at the same time. The game was used to train people in an army. A large field was needed for so many horses.

You have a long mallet in your hand. A mallet is a long stick with a head shaped like a cylinder. It is made of wood. In polo, you may only hold the mallet in your right hand. It keeps you from hitting other horses or players. You want to hit a small ball on the ground. If you get it in a goal, your team will win. You can also score a point if a player on the other team breaks the rules.

A whistle blows. The first chukker is beginning. A chukker is the amount of time for play. Each chukker lasts seven minutes. A game can have two, four, or six chukkers.

Only two players from each team can go down the field. You are one of the players to go. You squeeze the horse with your knees and race down the field. You tell the horse where to go by using your knees and holding the reins. The reins are the straps around the horse's head. You are close to the ball. You hit it down the field. You pull your mallet back again. Taking careful aim, you shoot it toward the goal. The goalie cannot stop the ball. You score! You pet your horse. You turn back and trot toward your side of the field.

Go on to the next page.

Pony Play, p. 2

Circle the word or phrase that best completes each sentence.

1. There are _____ people on each polo team.
   a. two   **b.** four   **c.** six

2. Veterinarians are people who _____.
   a. make sure the players follow the rules
   b. take care of animals
   c. make the goals

3. In polo, players hit the balls with _____.
   a. long wooden mallets
   b. their knees
   c. the reins of the horses

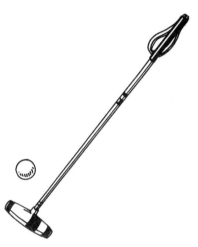

4. A chukker is _____.
   a. the amount of playing time
   b. when a player hits the ball into the goal
   c. a player who breaks the rules

5. Polo was used _____.
   a. to train horses for hunting
   b. so armies did not fight
   c. to train people in an army

6. A polo player tells the horse where to go by _____.
   a. squeezing with the knees
   b. using words
   c. letting go of the reins

Take Your Turn!
Who is Cecil Smith? Research to find out.

Going for the Gold

Good Sport

Team Helper

Team Player
of the Day

Team
Cheerleader

95

Answer Key

p. 10
1. b 2. a 3. c 4. a 5. c 6. a 7. b

p. 12
1. line 2. one 3. four 4. bounce 5. out 6. square
7. hands 8. walks

p. 14
1. c 2. a 3. a 4. c 5. c 6. b 7. a

p. 16
1. b 2. a. 3. c 4. c 5. a 6. b

p. 18
1. c 2. b 3. c 4. a 5. b 6. c 7. b

p. 20
Across 2. feet 4. arms 5. practice 6. tricks
Down 1. space 3. exercise 7. rope

p. 22
1. parachute 2. pie 3. mushroom 4. popcorn
5. Answers will vary.

p. 24
1. b 2. c 3. c 4. b 5. c 6. a 7. c

p. 26
1. a 2. c 3. b 4. a 5. a 6. b

p. 28
1. c 2. b 3. a 4. a 5. c 6. a

p. 30
1. pool 2. fish 3. pedals 4. tomato 5. Answers will
vary.

p. 32
1. b 2. c 3. a 4. b 5. c 6. c

p. 34
1. jump 2. track 3. meters 4. longest 5. javelin
6. fastest 7. kilograms 8. pole

p. 36
1. c 2. c 3. b 4. b 5. b 6. c

p. 38
1. a 2. c 3. b 4. c 5. c 6. b

p. 40
Across 3. youngest 5. Argentina 6. tennis
7. professional Down 1. won 2. fourteen 4. brother

p. 42
1. a 2. c 3. a 4. a 5. b 6. c 7. a

p. 44
1. four 2. beam 3. five 4. Russia 5. school 6. meet
7. elbow 8. medals

p. 46
1. hand 2. exercise 3. belt 4. kind 5. match 6. referee
7. judge 8. three

p. 48
1. c 2. a 3. c 4. b 5. c 6. b

p. 50
1. c 2. b 3. c 4. a 5. a 6. c

p. 52
Across 2. months 3. three 5. professional 6. lowest
Down 1. game 2. television 4. golfer

p. 54
1. c 2. a 3. a 4. b 5. b 6. a 7. c

p. 56
1. a 2. c 3. a 4. a 5. b 6. a

p. 58
1. pads 2. surfers 3. pools 4. wheels 5. deck 6. pipe
7. tricks 8. air

p. 60
1. a 2. c 3. a 4. b 5. a 6. b 7. a

p. 62
1. b 2. c 3. a 4. b 5. b 6. a

p. 64
1. a 2. c 3. a 4. b 5. a 6. b

p. 66
1. alley 2. pin 3. frame 4. road 5. Answers will vary.

p. 68
1. eleven 2. kick 3. coach 4. referee 5. tackle 6. four
7. pads 8. points

p. 70
Across 4. football 6. baseball 7. bottles 8. colleges
Down 1. throw 2. quarterback 3. Broncos 5. game

p. 72
1. c 2. b 3. a 4. b 5. a 6. b 7. a

p. 74
1. b 2. a 3. b 4. c 5. c 6. b

p. 76
1. b 2. a 3. a 4. b 5. b 6. a

p. 78
1. young 2. behave 3. priest 4. pitcher 5. batter
6. seven 7. Swat 8. Fame

p. 80
1. ball 2. field 3. goal 4. basketball 5. Answers will
vary.

p. 82
1. a 2. c 3. a 4. c 5. b 6. a

p. 84
1. c 2. a 3. b 4. b 5. b 6. a

p. 86
1. b 2. a 3. b 4. c 5. b 6. a

p. 88
1. b 2. c 3. a 4. a 5. c 6. a 7. c

p. 90
Across 2. sled 4. runners 6. ice 7. knees
Down 1. gloves 3. turns 5. slider

p. 92
1. b 2. a 3. c 4. a 5. a 6. b

p. 94
1. b 2. b 3. a 4. a 5. c 6. a